Mary Holm writes a personal fin[...]
Weekend Herald, presents a fortnightly financial segment on RNZ, and is a bestselling author and seminar presenter.

She has been a staff writer for the *New Zealand Listener*, a columnist in the *Dominion Post*, Christchurch *Press*, *Waikato Times* and other newspapers, business editor of the *Auckland Sun* and *Auckland Star*, and financial reporter for the *Australian Financial Review* and *Chicago Tribune*.

Her previous books include *Upside, Downside: A Guide to Risk for Savers and Investors* (Reserve Bank of New Zealand, 2012 and 2017); *The Complete KiwiSaver* (Random House, 2009); and *Get Rich Slow* (Penguin, 2006).

Mary holds an MBA in finance. She has been a lecturer at the University of Auckland, a member of the Savings Working Group and the Capital Markets Development Taskforce, and is a director of the Financial Markets Authority and Financial Services Complaints Ltd.

rich
enough?

A LAID-BACK GUIDE FOR EVERY KIWI

mary holm

HarperCollins*Publishers*

HarperCollins_Publishers_

First published in 2018
by HarperCollins_Publishers_ (New Zealand) Limited
Unit D1, 63 Apollo Drive, Rosedale, Auckland 0632, New Zealand
harpercollins.co.nz

Copyright © Mary Holm 2018

HarperCollins_Publishers_
Unit D1, 63 Apollo Drive, Rosedale, Auckland 0632, New Zealand
Level 13, 201 Elizabeth Street, Sydney NSW 2000, Australia
A 53, Sector 57, Noida, UP, India
1 London Bridge Street, London, SE1 9GF, United Kingdom
Bay Adelaide Centre, East Tower, 22 Adelaide Street West, 41st floor, Toronto, Ontario M5H 4E3, Canada
195 Broadway, New York NY 10007, USA

A catalogue record for this book is available from
the National Library of New Zealand

ISBN 978 1 7755 4133 2 (pbk)
ISBN 978 1 7754 9164 4 (ebook)

Cover design by Darren Holt, HarperCollins Design Studio
Cover images by shutterstock.com
Printed and bound in Australia by McPherson's Printing Group
The papers used by HarperCollins in the manufacture of this book are a natural, recyclable product made from wood grown in sustainable plantation forests. The fibre source and manufacturing processes meet recognised international environmental standards, and carry certification

To my son Tim (who told me about research that suggests happiness might actually decline beyond a certain income, and came up with some great ideas for this book – including having 'me days' as rewards); his partner Dom (who pointed out hard-to-follow sentences and out-of-date words and phrases like 'piddling', 'come a cropper' and 'skulduggery'); and to all of their young adult generation. May they understand that money is not what it's all about.

Contents

List of figures

Comments from readers of Mary's *Weekend Herald* column and books, and from listeners to her RNZ Your Money segment with Jesse Mulligan

'Thank you for opening my and many others' eyes to the often confusing world of investment.' – Ben E, landscape gardener, Whangarei

'I really *love* your column and I often discuss it with husband and 19-year-old, who is investing in shares – even though he is a poor student eating a lot of beans, flatting in another city. And yes he has KiwiSaver too! Keep writing and helping us all Mary. NZ needs you!' – Kim B, blogger, Thames

'I wanted to say a massive thank you for the effort you put into your column. Not so long ago I was in my early 20s and struggling under a mound of personal debt, but thanks to the advice in your column I managed to pay it all off and get into my first home before I turned 30.' – Ben S, economist, Auckland

'I have been listening to – and passing on – your advice to my kids and nieces and nephews for years – and really loved your book *Get Rich Slow* (which I gave away to someone who needed it more than me!). Keep up the brilliant work.' – Heather W, manager of her own rental properties, Auckland

'I'm an avid reader of your column. Thank you very much for your sage advice (and awesome comebacks) and great humour! Please keep educating us and making a difference for all Kiwis!' – Kai T, executive coach, Wellington

'As a member of the generation rent cohort I would like to thank you for making me feel that little bit better knowing that there are other ways to invest money other than property! ... Following your advice on RNZ, we have paid down all our debts, saved up our rainy day money of $15,000, and another $20,000 of savings too.' – Chloe K, self-employed, Auckland

'In July 2016 I changed my KiwiSaver investment to 80% balanced and 20% high growth (I was feeling brave after listening to you on the radio and reading your column!). I love your column and really enjoy listening to your spot on Jesse's program. Had I known in 2012 what I know now from you, I never would switched providers! Thank you for educating us all.' – Jill F, account manager, Tauranga

'I always enjoy your column, and your book *Get Rich Slow* helped us to get started, turning things around some years ago, so thank you.' – Graham S, self-employed, Auckland

'Thought I'd travel down memory lane with you. Back around 2001 you provided advice to us as we negotiated the dual pathways of co-parenting and tertiary education. Thanks to your advice, we adults attained many of our education goals, and the children (who are now nearing the end of high school) each have about $1,300 in a KiwiSaver account. My oldest (17) has just started part time work and is contributing 8% of weekly pay to the account. I'm thrilled to have my children so focused on saving for the future early in work life and that this will set them up well for the future.' – Joanne R, researcher, Auckland

'The first thing I do on a Saturday morning is read your column ... Recently my employer's superannuation fund wound up/paid out and they provided free professional independent financial advice for the beneficiaries. Before I met with the financial adviser I said to my wife, "I'm not going to be able to get through this meeting without saying at least once, 'But Mary Holm says ...'" By the end of the session with the adviser even *he* was saying, "Mary says ..."! Your advice is deeply appreciated and has helped us in unexpected ways in uncertain times. Your advice is garnished with kindness and thoughtfulness. Thank you for all you do. It makes a difference to people's lives.' – Dr Geoff N, lecturer, Otago

'Love your section in the Saturday *Herald* – best section in my opinion!' – Paula S, typist, Auckland

'Mary, I would like to thank you for your column. Thirteen years ago I separated from my husband and was left with my two young children to care for most of the time. I left with enough money for a deposit for my house and it is almost mortgage-free. Your column has educated me about sound financial decisions and all sorts of unexpected things I wouldn't have thought about. It's one of the reasons I buy the Saturday *Herald*!' – Anonymous

'I've lost count of the number of currency swings, economic downtowns, property slumps (and booms), even global financial meltdowns I've navigated thanks to your advice.' – Richard L, creative director, Auckland

'Thank you, Mary, your columns bring me confidence and comfort.' – Sherry C, Raglan

'When I was younger (I'm 27 now), I gave very little thought to how much I spent. If there was money in my bank account, then it was there to be spent – and it was! Thankfully, my money habits and financial decisions have become a bit more sensible in the past couple of years, in no small part due to the advice you have provided in your column.' – Marcus B, Wellington

'Keep up the great work. I know a lot of people who read your column and practice what you preach.' – Jacqui P, Auckland

'I moved to NZ nearly 16 years ago. Your columns, which are compulsive reading for me, are well researched and makes lot of sense all the time. I have followed your advice and have started investing in KiwiSaver for family and also started to look for local share market investment. I would like to thank you for your ongoing help through your columns and books.' – Pragnesh P, project manager, Auckland

'I wanted to write to say I am finding your booklet "Upside, Downside" absolutely brilliant! I am not business savvy or a financial guru, and you have explained everything so clearly and concisely that It's all making sense. I feel so enlightened! Thank you so much for sharing all your knowledge. It is very greatly appreciated.' – Greta H, radiographer, Christchurch

'My wife and I read your column every week and we very much appreciate the advice (as well as your sense of humour!)' – Anonymous, part retired, Auckland

AUTHOR'S NOTE: IS THIS BOOK FOR YOU?

You're worrying about your credit card debt, but hey, life's for living.

You've given up on ever owning a home.

You're wondering whether to wipe out your student loan.

You want to buy a car, but it's so hard to save for it.

Your mortgage is weighing you down – when will it *ever* be paid off?

You've heard about this low-risk investment that pays 20% – maybe you should try it?

You know bank term deposit interest is pathetic, but other investments seem too risky.

You've heard you need to save a million for retirement and that's just impossible.

You're dabbling in shares and seem to be pretty good at picking winners.

You've put all your savings in rentals because you can't go wrong with property.

You're retired and scared to put your savings in anything except the bank.

You've given KiwiSaver a miss, OR you're in but on a contributions holiday, OR you haven't got a clue if you're doing KiwiSaver right.

I'm here to help.

In many cases, I've been there myself. I've been poor (full-time student); somewhat richer (working); poor again (full-time student in the US); somewhat richer (working); poor-ish again (assets halved in divorce); somewhat richer again (working) …

I've been employed – by an oil company (for two days), a government department, big and little newspapers, big and little magazines; lost my job twice when newspapers folded; self-employed for 20 years …

I've lived and worked in New Zealand, London, small-town Michigan, Chicago, Sydney, New Zealand …

I've been married, divorced, a solo mum, a single middle-ager, single with a partner …

I've been a tenant, homeowner, landlord, tenant, homeowner, landlord again briefly … and a long-time investor in share funds.

And if I haven't done it myself, I've learnt about it from other New Zealanders.

Over the years I've received thousands – yes, literally thousands – of emails from readers of my *Weekend Herald* Q&A column and from listeners to my RNZ personal finance segment. I've discussed money issues with thousands of employees at workplace seminars, and thousands more students in university lectures. And I'm a voice for ordinary investors and consumers on the boards of the Financial Markets Authority and Financial Services Complaints Ltd.

I feel as if I know what worries New Zealanders about money, what they misunderstand, the mistakes they make – and their hopes and dreams.

And I know what I'm talking about – I hope! I hold a master of business administration degree in finance from one of the world's top business schools (the University of Chicago).

Most important of all, unlike many writers of finance books, I'm not selling any products or services (except this book!). I don't want to sign you up for costly advice or courses or investments. I just want you to do well.

I'm on *your* side.

At a party given by a billionaire – so the story goes – author Kurt Vonnegut tells his friend Joseph Heller that their host, a hedge-fund manager, had made more money in a *single day* than Heller had earned from his wildly popular novel *Catch-22* over its whole history. Heller responds, 'Yes, but I have something he will never have – enough.'

WHY DO YOU WANT TO BE RICHER?

Books about money and investing are full of info on *how* to boost your wealth. But I've never seen one that also asks '*why?*'.

At first that might seem a silly question. More money buys us more things and more experiences, and that adds up to more happiness, right?

Not necessarily. Lots of research shows that once we have a certain amount of money – enough to easily cover the basics and have some fun – having more doesn't necessarily make us happier. In fact, one recent study suggests that beyond a certain point, people with more money are less happy. More on this later in the book.

For five years I taught a course on financial literacy to non-Business School students at the University of Auckland. Worried that students might think my main message was 'the more money, the better', I asked every student to attend a discussion group where we looked into what made people happy, and the role of wealth in that.

Before coming to the class, the students were asked to do the following (which I dreamt up one day on a long drive). You might want to try it.

1. Write a list of eight individuals or couples you know well.
2. Give each one a score of 1 to 5 for wealth, with at least one getting a 1 and one getting a 5.
3. Give each one a score of 1 to 5 for happiness – again with at least one 1 and one 5.
4. See if the high scorers for wealth are also the high scorers for happiness.

Some students found the two were correlated – that wealthier people tended to be more content. But many saw no clear correlation, and every now and then someone saw the opposite – their poorer friends and relations tended to have a better time.

On balance, though, the students did tend to know more happy rich people than happy poor people. So is the research wrong?

Nick Powdthavee, a UK professor of behavioural science who looked at a great deal of research for his book *The Happiness Equation*, raises an intriguing question: Does wealth make us happier, or do happy people get wealthier? He found that happy people:

- tend to be more creative and productive
- have better health – which tends to lead to more wealth
- are more likely to be financially successful

It seems that happiness is more likely to lead to wealth than the other way around.

As Nobel Peace Prize winner Albert Schweitzer put it: 'Success is not the key to happiness. Happiness is the key to success. If you love what you are doing, you will be successful.'

If you start out with a happy disposition, there's a good chance you'll end up well off. If you start out grumpy, you're less likely to do well financially. Of course, you might get lucky with money, but it's unlikely to change your outlook on life.

So where does this leave you, as you're starting to read a book about investing? Why try to get richer if it probably won't make you happier?

Check back to what I said above. While wealth and happiness don't seem to be highly correlated after you've got the basics well covered, many of you will feel you haven't covered all the basics yet.

Nobody would argue that if you're struggling to cut credit card debt, or to get together a deposit for a modest first home, or to save up enough to do some fun things in retirement, having a few more bucks wouldn't be welcome.

Even if you're financially comfortable, more money gives you more choices. These might include supporting others, from family members to charities.

So, while it may not make sense to put lots of time, effort and worry into absolutely maximising your wealth, it does make sense to take a few straightforward steps to make your money work better for you.

Read this book, take the steps that apply to you, and you'll have the money stuff sorted. You can then spend less time working and more time getting on with things that will really improve your wellbeing.

What might that be? At the end of the book, we'll look a little further into some of the fascinating research about what makes people happy. But for now, let's get on with making you financially strong enough to make the most of your life.

Step
1
START NOW – IT'S EASY

In which we ...

- Observe that laid-back investing is good
- Compare savvy Sally and slow Suzy
- Also compare the apprentice and the graduate
- See that you'll have a lot more than twice as much if you save for 40 years instead of 20
- Learn that compounding is a friend for savers, a foe for those in debt
- Discard those 'You need a million dollars' messages

People often ask me if I've read the latest book about the share market or investing. 'No', I reply. 'There are too many good novels to read. Besides, a lot of what's written about investing isn't much good, and sometimes it's actually a big worry. It can persuade readers to take steps that will do them more harm than good.'

When it comes to investing, laziness is good.

That might sound crazy. In pretty much everything else we do – from running marathons to getting promoted fast at work to mastering the piano to creating a magical garden – the more work we put into it the better we'll do.

But investing is different.

We all know people who put hours into their investments. They read the financial pages, and listen to the economists who tell them – more like guess, actually – what's likely to happen in the next year. Then they read about which investments have done well lately. On the strength of that they choose which shares or bonds to buy or sell, and when to buy or sell them.

And guess what? Most of them end up with less than you will after you've read this book, set up your investments and got on with other things. It's sometimes called 'Set and forget'.

Let's not be misleading here. I'm not saying you should never do anything after the initial set-up. Every few years it's a good idea to do a quick review of your investments. But the changes you might make are easy – half-hour sort of stuff. There'll be more about this in Step 6: 'Stay cool', but for now, let's look at the basics.

Three ways to get more savings

It's quite simple, really. The three ways to get more savings are:

1. Earn more.
2. Save more.
3. Be smarter with what you do with your savings.

Of course, it's also great to get a pay rise – either in your current job or by starting a new job.

During my extended OE in the United States, I still recall the excitement of moving from a small-town Michigan newspaper, the wonderfully named *Jackson Citizen Patriot*, to the *Chicago Daily News*. The pay rise meant less than the thrill of knowing I would work with some great journalists. But still, my pay went from something like $US14,000 to $US21,000 a year – not to be sneezed at back then when a dollar was worth a dollar.

Chances are you will get at least one huge pay jump in your life. Fantastic! But that's not what this book is about. It's not what you earn, but how much you save that matters. And, perhaps more importantly, what really matters is *how* you save.

> **Key message:** You don't have to earn a lot to become wealthy. I'll show you how to get much more mileage out of what money you have.

Get going

I know the feeling. Practical friends tell me I should get the runners on the sliding door to my deck fixed. I don't understand much about things like that, and I don't know who to ask, and it all gets too hard and doesn't happen.

Maybe you feel that way about your finances. The 'Don't Know and Don't Know Who to Trust' syndrome finds us doing nothing, week after week, year after year.

With my house, it might matter if it all starts falling apart. With your money, there are no 'ifs'. It *will* matter. Muck around for a year or two and you can end up retiring with much, much less.

But don't panic! This book will teach you how to invest your money. It's not hard – I promise.

Okay, let's get on with it. Sure, you're allowed to read this book right through first. (Kind, aren't I!) But please don't delay after that. Sitting on the sidelines for just a couple of years can make a surprisingly big difference. Think world trip in retirement versus the South Island. Oops! The Mainlanders are grumbling. I've got nothing against the South Island – I have done some wonderful tramps there – but it's not quite Venice.

Let's look at Sally and Suzy, 22-year-old twins earning $40,000 each. Sally joins KiwiSaver now, but Suzy is busy with other stuff, and joins when she's 25. Even if they stick with just middle-risk funds – and I will be encouraging you to be braver – at 65, Sally is likely to have a bit more than $600,000. Suzy will have just over $500,000.

There's just three years' difference in the starting point – during which Sally put in 3% of her pay, or about $1,200 a year. But at the other end she has more than $100,000 extra. Wow! The contributions from her employer and the government plus the growth of her savings over many years have worked wonders.

We should note that by the time the twins retire, $100,000 won't mean as much as it does today, because of inflation. But still, it will buy more than a few good cups of coffee.

A 2017 BERL (Business and Economic Research Ltd) report illustrates the importance of starting early. It compared how well off people are at retirement, depending on whether they:

- left high school and got no further qualification;
- became an apprentice; or
- got a degree at university.

Predictably, the high-school leaver was worse off at the end of their career. But the other two ended up about equal at retirement, despite the fact that towards the end of their careers the graduate earned close to $100,000 while the apprentice earned around $80,000.

Tradespeople earn significantly more than graduates at the beginning of their careers, which means they put more into KiwiSaver in the early years. Also, they have no student loans to repay, and they are able to buy a home earlier and pay off the mortgage sooner. 'This, combined with sensible investment, compounds into significant wealth,' says BERL.

> **Key message:** Starting to save early, and paying off debt as soon as possible, makes a big difference over the long haul.

Figure 1: Start now!
Saving $100 a month

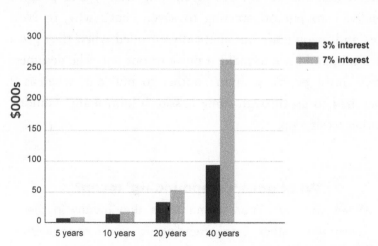

Source: Reserve Bank of NZ

Figure 1 shows us two things:

- If you save for 10 years you'll accumulate more than twice as much as you would over 5 years. At 20 years it's more than twice the 10-year total. And at 40 years it's way more than twice the 20-year total. This is because of compounding growth (explained below).
- You save a lot more if you earn 7% interest than if you earn 3%. And the longer you save, the bigger that difference is.

Note that Figure 1 is not about KiwiSaver savings, but just ordinary money-in-the-bank type savings. In KiwiSaver, if you contribute $100 a month, your savings will grow much more because of government contributions, plus employer contributions if you're an employee. (More on that in Step 4: 'Join the best KiwiSaver fund for you'.)

Let's just note here that the designers of KiwiSaver understood the advantages of starting now – and people's tendency to put off starting to save. That's why, in New Zealand, people are automatically enrolled when they get a new job, and have to make a move to opt out. The designers knew most people wouldn't bother to pull out, whereas if they had to go through some hassle to join, many wouldn't bother to sign up.

What does 'compounding' mean?

When you earn interest and leave that money in the investment rather than spending it, you'll then earn interest on that interest as well as on your original money.

In turn, that new lot of interest will earn interest on interest – and on it goes. It makes your savings grow at an increasing rate.

You might start with $100, which grows in a year to $110. But in the next year it might grow to $121, then $133 the following year, then $146, $161, $177, $195 and so on. Each jump is bigger than the one before.

Compounding is a great friend when you're saving – but a great enemy if your debt is compounding.

True tale: Give it time

The sale of a house in St Marys Bay, Auckland, in 2018 shows the power of long-term compounding growth. A family had owned the house since 1900, when they bought it for 400 pounds – equivalent to $800, the *New Zealand Herald* reports. They sold it for $3 million.

That sounds like an extraordinary gain. But it translates into growth of just 7.2% a year.

> **Moral:** A fairly ordinary annual gain over a long enough period can translate into a huge number.

You don't need a million

I've read in so many places that you need to retire with a million dollars – over and above the value of your home. Nonsense! Stop to think about who is saying that. It's nearly always fund managers, bank managers, stockbrokers, financial advisers – anyone in the long list of people who make a buck out of your saving with them.

And it makes me angry. I suppose it encourages some people to save – although in some cases they might over-save (something we'll look into in Step 5: 'Boost your saving painlessly'). But I suspect that for every person who is inspired to save more by that message, there are five others who say to themselves, 'This is hopeless. I'll be lucky to save $100,000. I might as well just give up.'

One of the features of setting goals that work – more about that in our next step – is that they have to be *realistic goals*. Aim for the moon and you end up in your own back yard. Aim for the top of a nearby hill and you might well get there.

The fact is that you don't need a million dollars to have a pleasant retirement. As I said at the start, once you've got a certain amount of money, more doesn't necessarily make you happier.

For the person who might have retired with no savings, having $30,000 or $50,000 in KiwiSaver is a big plus – a few delicious retirement treats. Their neighbour might aspire to $300,000 to $500,000 or more. That's cool. Use this book to make the most of your savings, and don't get caught up in comparing amounts with your friends, neighbours or anyone else.

This is about your money. You know what numbers are realistic for you. I hope I can raise your horizons – and for some of you that will indeed be to a million dollars and beyond. But for many, a million bucks is silly. This book is for you, too.

Actually, it's especially for you. You have the most to gain.

True tale: Cruising with $600,000

An encouraging story from a married couple:

'We two worried like hell about the same stuff as everybody else, well before and indeed after we retired, which was ten years ago now. We started retirement with $600,000, the result of 20 years of saving – way less than the $1 million being bandied about.

'We decided to leave only our mortgage-free house to our lovely children and enjoy the rest. We have travelled extensively but economically in these first 10 years, knowing that we will almost certainly slow down in the next decade or so. It has been a truly fabulous experience, and we still live very comfortably with more than half our initial capital remaining.

'As you advise, we have invested productively in shares for the long term, and laddered bonds and term investments for the near- to medium-term future. We have upskilled, and done this ourselves with no involvement of high-priced advisers, and yes, we've lost some but gained more.

'We currently live on $52,000 a year after tax, made up of Super, investment earnings and by eating some of our capital. We expect to be solely on NZ Superannuation when we are 87, which is fine by us.

'A decent retirement is possible. It takes work, persistence, a bit of luck, not being put off by the big numbers, while listening to, and acting on, good advice.'

There'll be more about investing in shares, laddering bonds, and investing in retirement later in the book.

Moral: You can do it, too!

Step 1 check

Have you:

- ❏ Promised yourself that you will start saving – or beef up your saving – *now*?
- ❏ Set your sights on a reasonable savings goal for you?

Reward

As you complete each step in this book, give yourself a little treat. It should cost less than $50, ideally much less or nothing. The idea is to come up with something that you don't normally get for yourself, something that says, 'Well done, you!'

In the supermarket you might buy – for once – the best chocolates or cheese or flowers. Or you might book yourself a 'me day' to do something you really want to do but never find time for. That could be going for a walk, reading a book, spending time with family, having a picnic, going to the beach, trying something creative ... Or what about donating to a charity you care about? Research shows that giving brings pleasure for the giver as well as the recipient.

If a step has been particularly tough, your reward might be something you can look at again and again, to remind yourself of what you've achieved – a picture or a piece of jewellery. Whatever makes you smile.

What's next? The step that may change your financial situation more than any other.

Step
2

KILL OFF HIGH-INTEREST DEBT

In which we ...

- Look at the only good, high-paying, risk-free 'investment'
- Plot to stop the banks from making big profits on credit cards
- Work out what to do with Auntie Mabel's legacy
- Learn what's so SMART about setting a goal
- Examine why you spend, and consider whether you really know what you spend on
- Work out how to get more trips, cars and toys
- Find out how to be a credit card winner
- Listen to a plea about student loans

Psst! Have I got an investment for you! No, we need more exclamation marks. Have I got an investment for you!!!! It's easy! And it pays you 20% a year!! At no risk!!!

I hope you're looking at me sideways. 'What's Mary up to? This is definitely too good to be true.' That's exactly how I would want you to respond to any 'low-risk' investment offering more than very low interest.

But this is different.

Oops! I hope you're looking at me even more askance. The 'this time it's different' line should make all the warning lights flash.

So what am I on about? Paying off high-interest debt.

I *hate* seeing people with expensive debt – often run up on credit cards, or to buy a car or computer or something. (To keep things simple, we'll call it all credit card debt.)

Most credit cards are run by banks, and they must love people with big card debt. Banks take in people's money – in savings accounts and term deposits – and these days they pay pretty low interest on it. And they lend money out – for mortgages, business loans and credit card purchases – and charge higher interest on it, especially on cards.

To some extent that's fair enough. They've got to cover the costs of running the business, and losses on loans that aren't paid back. They've also got to give profits to their owners, the shareholders. But those profits are awfully big these days.

In light of that, I can't see how banks can justify charging around 20% on credit card debt. But they often do.

And people pay. According to credit scoring company CreditSimple, one in three New Zealanders doesn't pay off their credit card in full each month, which means they pay hugely high interest on the balance. Presumably most make the minimum required payment, which is a con. If that's all you pay, your debt is likely to grow rather than shrink even if you make no more purchases.

And it gets worse. More than one in ten said in a survey that they're comfortable with credit card debt of up to $10,000. Horrors!

Let's start, right now, on a campaign to deprive banks of the profits they make on credit cards. How? Don't pay their high interest rates by not having the debt in the first place. Too late for you? Well let's get rid of it.

You'll be in good company. In a New Zealand survey conducted a couple of years ago, nearly three-quarters of the people said they are concentrating on reducing and minimising their debt.

What 20% amounts to

In the last step, we talked about compounding. If you have a 20% credit card debt, and don't pay it off, the compounding can be truly frightening.

Let's say you owe $1,000 and make no payments. After a year you'll owe $1,200. The next year it will be $1,440, then $1,728, then $2,074. The debt has more than doubled in just four years.

The year after that it's $2,488, then $2,986, $3,583, $4,300, $5,160. After nine years, your $1,000 debt is more than five times as big. That's horrible.

Are you a lucky one?

If you've got credit card or similar debt that you don't expect to pay off on the next bill, in an odd sort of way you're lucky! You can take advantage of that 20% 'investment' – or thereabouts – touted at the start of this step.

How does that work? Let's start by considering how we measure financial wealth. We could look at the things somebody owns – properties, cars, shares, whatever. But what if a big spender has borrowed to the hilt to buy those items? His debts might even be bigger than the value of his assets.

That might not matter for a while. But what say he loses his job, or his business founders in a downturn, and he needs to sell some assets to buy the groceries and clothe the kids? Because the economy has slumped, others are in a similar plight, so there are lots of properties, cars and shares on the market, going cheap.

Desperate to sell, our hero accepts low prices. In an extreme case, he might find himself with no assets to speak of but still owing money to the bank. Wealthy that ain't!

A true measure of our wealth is the value of our assets *minus* our debts.

In a fascinating book called *The Millionaire Next Door*, Thomas J. Stanley and William D. Danko draw on their research on American millionaires. They found that most professional people *looked* wealthy, judging by their homes, cars, clothes and lifestyles. But many were like our big spender. They had borrowed heavily to live that way. Subtract their debt from their assets and there wasn't much wealth left.

Stanley and Danko found that many of the actual millionaires were the folk next door, who had lived in the same nice but ordinary house for decades, often ran small businesses, and kept their debt low.

So what's all this got to do with you? To keep it simple, we'll say you have:

- Assets: long-term bank deposits of $30,000.
- Debts: $10,000 of credit card debt.

As we said above, your wealth – sometimes called your net worth – is your assets minus your debts. So your net worth is:

$30,000 – $10,000 = $20,000

One day you hear that your sweet old Auntie Mabel – bless her – has died and left you $5,500. What do you do with it? Firstly, you blow $500 on a party or a weekend away. Life is for living, and not every penny needs to be spent sensibly! But should you put the remaining $5,000 into term deposits or pay down debt?

If you put it in term deposits, your assets will grow to $35,000. So your assets minus debts look like this:

$35,000 – $10,000 = $25,000

If you use it to reduce your credit card debt, it will fall to $5,000. So we have:

$30,000 – $5,000 = $25,000

> **Key message:** Reducing your debt has the same effect on your wealth as adding to your savings.

So which is better? Here's where it gets interesting, or should we say interest-ing? Look at:

- The interest you could earn if you put the $5,000 into a term deposit. We'll say it's 2% after tax.
- The interest you will avoid paying if you put the $5,000 into paying off the credit card debt. Let's say 20%.

The choice is obvious. It's far better to reduce 20% debt than add to 2% term deposits.

In fact, reducing 20% debt boosts your wealth as much as adding an investment that pays you 20%. No sound investment can promise 20% without big risk, but reducing debt is risk-free. It's a no-brainer 'investment' for anyone with high-interest debt.

A couple of quick points.

The first point is that when I said you're lucky for having this debt, I didn't really mean it! You're actually unlucky, to put it charitably. Many would say you're stupid, but I'm not that mean. Whatever we call you, it's not clever to have high-interest debt. You'll often end up paying twice as much – or more – for something because of all the interest you pay. You're lucky only in the sense that you've done something so bad that changing it will be so good!

The second point is for anyone wondering how mortgages fit into this. A mortgage is certainly debt. But it's a far cry from credit card debt for a couple of reasons: the interest rate is much lower; and you're buying an asset that will almost always grow in value over the years.

Still, it's a good idea to get rid of a mortgage quickly, too. (For more on this, see 'Reducing a mortgage' (page 260) in Step ?: 'Buy a home, or sell one'.)

True tale: They owed $180,000, now it's zero

A reader wrote to my *Weekend Herald* Q&A column:

'[About ten years ago] my then-wife and I had racked up close to $180,000 on credit card and personal loan debt over the preceding six years.

'How did it happen? Relying on up to eight credit cards as an easy fix for everyday spending when times were tough, when unemployment struck, or simply to survive as a family with young kids. And using credit rather than saving up and only buying what we had cash for.

'How did it get to that level? Credit card companies saw us as easy targets, with regular increased credit limits, new flash credit cards sent to us every six months, and the monthly balancing act of cash advances from one credit card to pay the minimum due for another card.

'How did we get out of it? Only through the help of a financially literate friend who negotiated with our debtors and helped us to freeze interest payments, reach full and final settlements, and put in the sheer hard work of paying off more than $150,000.

'Result – debt-free, able to buy back into the property market, and the freedom that can only come with being out of the mercenary grip of banks, financial institutions and debt collectors.'

It's a wonderfully encouraging letter for others in a similar situation.

Thank goodness the couple's friend came to their aid. Others who don't have such a friend should contact FinCap (previously called the National Building Financial Capability Charitable Trust) (www.fincap.org.nz). Through them, you can get the same sort of help as the friend provided.

Moral: You can get rid of huge debt if you really want to.

Setting a goal

Winners in life set goals – and achieve them. It might be to get top of the class in history, win a half marathon, lose 5 kilograms … Or slay credit card debt.

Goals that work are SMART:

- Specific – your goal might be to get rid of your Visa card debt. If you've got more than one card with debt, start with the one that charges the highest interest rate.
- Measurable – you'll reduce it by $100 a week.
- Achievable – you're confident you can free up that amount for repayments. If you're not confident, reduce it – although try to at least cover the interest you're being charged, or you're going backwards.
- (W)ritten – put it on a piece of paper and stick it on the fridge door.
- Time-bound – plan to pay it off in two years from now.

You're not happy with putting the goal on the fridge, where all your friends can ask you about it? Get happy. Research shows that if you tell others about your goal, you're more likely to achieve it. That makes sense – you don't want to look like a failure.

But if you do slip up occasionally, don't be hard on yourself. You're human. And don't say, 'I didn't pay off any last week, so I'll make it $200 this week.' That gets too hard. Just pick up where you left off.

A few further tips on making your goal work:

- Set up automatic payments from your bank account the day after your income goes in.

- Add extra payments whenever you can.
- Give yourself little rewards when you reach, say, a quarter of your goal, then half, three-quarters and the whole lot. But no putting the rewards on your credit card!

By the way – on that bit about telling your friends your goals – here's something else to think about. If you find yourself *not* telling family or friends about a purchase you've made, because you're worried they'll think it's silly or extravagant, that suggests it wasn't a good purchase. Before making future purchases, ask yourself if you will be happy to tell others about them.

An emailed reminder

You can send a message to yourself at a future date at www.futureme.org. An email will come into your inbox on the date you nominated – which has to be at least a month later. It's free, and it's a good way to see if you are on track with your goal.

Pay off more

Figure 2 shows that doubling your credit card debt repayments way more than halves the total interest you pay and the time to pay off the debt. And paying off three times as much is even better.

Try the Debt Calculator on www.sorted.org.nz with your own numbers to see just how effective a quicker payoff can be.

Figure 2: Increasing credit card payments helps hugely

Payments on $5,000 debt at 20% interest

Monthly payments	Total interest paid	Time to pay off
$100	$5,840	9 years 1 month
$200	$1,522	2 years 9 months
$300	$906	1 year 8 months

Source: Debt Calculator on www.sorted.org.nz

The psychology of spending

You've set a goal to get rid of your credit card debt. Now let's understand why you ran up that debt in the first place – and how you might prevent that from happening again.

If you're always running up credit card and other debt, you're spending too much – by definition.

As Charles Dickens's character Mr Micawber said, 'Annual income twenty pounds, annual expenditure nineteen [pounds] nineteen [shillings] and six [pence], result happiness. Annual income twenty pounds, annual expenditure twenty pounds ought and six, result misery.'

Why do you do it? Because you want stuff and experiences. They make you feel happy at the time.

Think about it, though. Once the new jacket has been in your wardrobe for a few months, or the memory of the meal has faded, you're often no happier than before you spent that money. You bought a short-term glow with long-term gloom.

I'm not saying that applies to every purchase. We can all look back on certain holidays or concerts with great pleasure, or point to items in our homes that we've loved for years.

But those are the standouts. So much of what we buy just becomes the new ordinary.

Next time you buy a treat, note in your diary to assess a month later – and a year later – if the purchase has made you happier.

Another reason you might spend more money than you have is to keep up appearances. Your friends have certain clothes, cars, holidays, whatever. You don't want to look like the poor relation. But think about it. Do your friends care if you don't 'meet the standards'? If yes, how genuine is the friendship?

Some of the professional people written about in *The Millionaire Next Door* had put themselves under huge stress to look good. It's a pretty stupid way to live your life.

Back in 2008, the Families Commission said in its Beyond Reasonable Debt report that a person is more likely to get into debt if they:

- feel they are not in control of their own life and actions
- base their aspirations on comparison with others
- have poor self-control and a tendency to be impulsive

I doubt if that has changed.

I spend about um ...

Here's a trick. Write down estimates of how much you spend in different categories. They might include: food, clothes, transport, housing, entertainment and so on. Then keep track of your actual spending for a month or two. Where there's a big difference between the estimate and the actual spending, that suggests where you could cut back.

Warning: You might learn something you don't like! An Australian study found that most people estimated their spending on transport and rent fairly accurately. But they spent more than they thought on clothes, considerably more on booze, and way more on gambling. Funny that.

The Christmas trap

Christmas – and the holiday that often follows – mean credit card spending often gets out of control.

A 2017 survey found that 15% of New Zealanders have more than 11 people on their Christmas list to shop for. And about 27% (more often women) said they planned to spend over $200 per child on presents. Meanwhile 15% (more often men) were spending more than $200 on their partners.

In sum, 17% expected their total household spend on Christmas to be more than $1,000 – on food, travel, presents and decorations.

It's hardly surprising that late credit card payments reach their peak in January, February and March each year.

Ask yourself: Do you really enjoy buying, giving and receiving, or is the family gathering more important? Are children happier with more presents but stressed parents?

Other ways to do it:

- Draw names out of hat and each person gives to just that family member whose name they have drawn.
- Set a low dollar limit for presents.
- Give to the kids only, and teens get $20 each.
- Switch to giving presents for birthdays only. Make a bigger deal of each person's birthday.
- Family members all put money into a charity.

Free up time and energy to concentrate on good (but not necessarily expensive) food, and the family having a fun time together.

The power of habits

If you examine your spending, you'll probably find that a lot of it is habitual. You always buy your lunch on workdays, or get a new outfit when you're going to a party, or eat out at pricier places. But here's the encouraging bit:

> **Key message:** If you want to change a habit, you need to do the new behaviour for just one month.

That's a lot easier to take on than thinking about struggling for a lifetime to do something different. I've tried it for all sorts of things, from alcohol-free days to taking get-fit walks. And it works! (There's an excellent three-minute TED talk on this at www.tinyurl.com/30DaysTED)

Throughout this book you'll see links that start 'www.tinyurl.com'. That's not the name of the website! I use tinyurl to make links much shorter than they really are, so it's easier for you to type them in.

Tip: Research has shown that you're much more likely to form a new habit if you reward yourself *every time* you do the right thing, at least at the start. For something frequent, you might just mark off a card, and every time you get ten marks you can do X. Each mark will feel like a reward. Changing bad habits is more complicated, but consistent rewards still make a big difference.

If your habit not only costs you money but harms your health – such as spending on cigarettes, booze or fast food – when you change it you kill two birds with one stone. Terrific!

On the good habits side of the ledger, a *really* good one is to always save up before you buy that car or trip or electronic toy, so you can buy it with cash.

If you usually take an overseas holiday on your credit card and pay it off many months later, decide that for just one year you'll do a cheaper trip within New Zealand, and save for it first. Right after that trip, you can start saving for next year's overseas trip, using money that otherwise would have gone to credit card payments. By the time you take your next trip, you can pay for it with cash. And continue to do that year after year. For the sake of just one less exciting holiday, you've saved thousands of dollars of interest over the years.

By saving first, you make interest your friend – because you earn interest on your savings – instead of the enemy that doubles your debt or worse. The end result is that over a lifetime you can afford to buy many more cars, trips and toys – or perhaps help your grandchild to get through university.

What's more, you can often get a better price on something like an appliance or computer if you tell the salesperson you're paying with cash.

The other advantage of saving up first is that it gives you time to think about whether you really want to buy that item. Which brings me to another point: often, if you put off a purchase decision for a day, or even just a few hours, in a different place, perhaps with different people, you might come to your senses and realise you don't need to make that purchase!

You probably don't deserve it

I confess to being caught up by this line. An ad says I should buy something because I deserve it, or have earned it. Of course I know they're conning me. I might have been lying around doing nothing. But if I want to justify buying an item I can always come up with *something* I've done lately that makes me feel like a good person.

It's a clever line, and I'm sure I'm not the only one sucked in. Watch out for it – and all the other lines that advertisers and marketers come up with to 'get' you. Think about how they are manipulating your mind, and get them out of there. What you actually deserve is a decent retirement.

A couple of other traps:

- Cash back. You're borrowing $15,000 to buy a car, and the lender offers you $16,000. It doesn't seem like much more debt, and it would be great to have $1,000 to blow on fun over the next couple of weeks. Don't be tempted!
- Buy now, regret later. It's becoming easier and easier to buy items online on a 'buy now, pay later' basis, and recent research shows that many people using this service don't look at the terms and conditions, which could include high interest or harsh penalties if you don't pay on time. Users have told researchers, 'I just clicked.' Don't.

What about the *unlucky* lucky ones?

Some of you might have got angry reading this step. It wasn't spending on fun that left you with lots of high-interest debt, but a financial crunch.

Maybe you lost your job and found it hard to get another. Maybe your car needed major unexpected repairs and you need a car to get to work. Maybe your small business didn't turn out as planned. Or you needed unexpected house repairs. Or you had a medical problem and didn't want to go on a waiting list to solve it. Or you felt you had to leave your partner, even though that would cause severe financial difficulties. Maybe …

We all have bills we expect. The electricity might cost more this month, but the bill is still 'within the ball park'. But we all also get bills that come out of the blue. And they're the ones that lead people to run up big debt in crisis situations. If that's you, you have my sympathy – but also my encouragement to get that debt off your shoulders.

You have the following choices:

- Go through life telling anyone who will listen that luck has been against you and that's why you're struggling.
- Set yourself a goal and get back on the financially winning side.

Which one is going to make you happier? And your friends? Nobody likes listening to someone else's woes. Sorry, but whatever sad story you tell me, I've probably heard a sadder one from someone who got out of the hole. You can, too.

Free help

If you want help with controlling your spending, go to FinCap's website, www.fincap.org.nz.

It says there, 'Budgeting services offer free, confidential budgeting advice. With a financial mentor, you can create a plan to get out of debt, save money and start building a future for you and your family.'

The mentors might, for example, talk to the people and companies you owe money, to stop interest from growing while you set up a repayment plan that's workable for you. They might also help you convert high-interest debt to a low- or no-interest loan, or even get some debt forgiven.

You can find a service near you, and there are also resources on the website, such as a budget worksheet, cashflow sheet, debt schedule, and financial plan of action.

Be a credit card winner

Some books tell people who run up big credit card debt to cut up their card and don't get another one. But that seems too negative. Credit cards can be really useful. For example, if your car breaks down and you need it to get to work – and there's no public transport or friends going that way – using a credit card for the repairs gives you a month or so to come up with the cash, before you have to pay the credit card bill. So I would rather see you become a credit card winner.

Winners never pay a lick of interest on their cards. They actually gain a little bit by using their card. That's because they delay paying for items for a month or so, until the credit card bill due date. In the meantime, the money they would have spent is sitting in the bank earning a little interest. This is sometimes over-rated in these days of low interest. But the interest bonus probably more than covers the annual card fee, if you don't get one of those expensive cards.

And winners get the main benefit of using a credit card – convenience.

Here's how to be a winner:

- Set up payments to come automatically out of your bank account on the days when card payments are due.
- Put a note in your diary or on a calendar a couple of days before each due date to make sure there's enough in the bank account to pay the bill.
- Make sure you always have that money available – perhaps in a savings account. If you haven't, you've overspent on your card. You're back with the credit card losers. Don't let it happen twice!

By the way, it's also wise to set up automatic payments of your electricity, insurance and other regular bills. Getting behind with payments and paying interest or penalties isn't clever.

Two ways to help you slay credit card debt

Take a holiday
No, no! I don't mean flying off to somewhere warm and putting it all on your card. We've got rid of that behaviour, remember?

This is about a KiwiSaver contributions holiday (which will probably be called a 'savings suspension' from April 2019). As you'll see in Step 4: 'Join the best KiwiSaver fund for you', I'm a pretty big fan of the scheme. But I hate high-interest debt more than I love KiwiSaver. Hence this plan.

If you're in KiwiSaver and you're struggling to get rid of a large credit card debt, take a contributions holiday. It's easy to apply online at www.tinyurl.com/ContribHoliday.

However, this is okay only if you use all the extra take-home income to pay down your debt. Set up an automatic transfer from your bank account to do that. And set up a plan to increase your debt payments a little every month.

While you're doing this, you're missing out on the KiwiSaver incentives, so you want to get the debt down to zero just as fast as possible.

Promise yourself that as soon as the debt is paid off, you'll restart your KiwiSaver contributions. If your contributions holiday is still running, you can always cut it short. Just ask your employer to start making deductions from your pay again.

Add to your mortgage

If your house is worth a fair bit more than your mortgage, ask the lender if you can add to the mortgage and use that money to pay off your high-interest debt.

Keep in mind, though, that you're still paying interest on that amount – just at a lower rate. So please arrange to pay off that extra mortgage money fast. If you just let it become part of your long-term mortgage, you could end up paying more interest on the money over the years than you saved.

What about payday loans?

If you have borrowed money from payday lenders – the ones who give you money for a short period, perhaps to tide you over until your next payday – my arguments in this step are even stronger.

With a typical payday loan, you might borrow $200 to pay an overdue power bill, and have to repay it in a week or two. The interest and other costs might amount to $20. While this may not seem much, if you can't repay the loan the interest and fees will compound, turning into a horrific annual interest rate. Rates of around 800% are not uncommon in New Zealand.

No wonder the people offering payday loans seem so friendly. They're making out like bandits – and you're the victim. Get rid of debt like this as fast as possible. And get yourself into a situation in which you'll never glance at payday lending again. How? See the next step.

True tale: How $800 debt turned into more than $2,000 in just 7 months

A case study on the website of Financial Services Complaints Ltd (FSCL), one of four New Zealand financial dispute resolution schemes, tells the story of 21-year-old William, who earns $42,000 a year.

One August, William borrowed $800 from payday lender Phone for Cash. He was told he would have to repay $1,264 within 45 days. His debt was multiplied by more than one and a half in just a month and a half!

When William didn't repay the loan, the company started trying to recover the money. By October, the debt totalled $1,372, and by November it was $1,586 – almost double what he had borrowed just three months before.

'Phone for Cash asked William to see a budget adviser,' says FSCL. 'The budget adviser said William could afford to pay $75 a week. Phone for Cash said this was not enough, and wanted William to pay $600 a week. William phoned FSCL in March. By now his debt was $2,070.'

FSCL tried to help William and the company negotiate a settlement. 'Phone for Cash was not prepared to accept

$75 a week from William. It was barely enough to keep pace with the interest, and Phone for Cash was concerned William would again default.'

The dispute was finally resolved when William repaid the debt in full – possibly by borrowing from his father.

Moral: Stay away from payday lenders!

How do student loans fit into all this?

Student loans are a worry. Let's not get into whether or not it's fair that students pay for a portion of their tertiary education. There are strong arguments on both sides – but that's for another day. What is clearly a concern, though, is that you may have run up a student loan of tens of thousands of dollars, sometimes more, and that might have affected your attitude to debt.

Student loans are 'good' debt. By borrowing, you've been able to further your education. And research shows that most people with higher qualifications earn more money in the long run. Nor is it all about money. Good tertiary education opens your mind to other ways of looking at life, and gives you all sorts of social and cultural opportunities.

Other examples of good loans are borrowing to buy a home or anything else you expect will grow in value over time.

'Bad' borrowing, on the other hand, is borrowing to buy things that decrease in value. It's what we've been talking about – high-interest credit card debt and similar.

Please, please don't think that because your student loan is big, it won't make much difference if you run up a bit more debt to buy fun things. Don't mix up good and bad debt.

Okay, off your soapbox, Mary!

Let's look at whether paying off a student loan faster than you have to is similar to paying off credit card debt.

If you live in New Zealand, your student loan is interest-free. So when we're making our comparison, it will be between:

- the interest you could earn if you put money into an investment – say 2% after tax in a term deposit or more in other investments; and
- the interest you will avoid paying if you used the money to pay down your student loan – which is zero.

The student loan is always going to be the loser. While many people want to get the student loan monkey off their back – and I can understand that – it doesn't make financial sense to repay it faster than the compulsory repayments that come out of your pay. It's better to put any extra money into some kind of saving or investment.

Sure, the bank will take note of your student loan when they're considering you for a mortgage. The lower it is, the better. But they'll also take note of the savings you've made. And your savings will have grown faster than the student loan would have fallen, because of compounding interest.

If you live overseas, the situation is different. You pay interest on your student loan, in 2018–19, at 4.3%. While you may be able to earn more than that, after-tax, on some investments, they will be fairly risky. If you're not living in New Zealand, it's a great idea to make a priority of paying off your student loan as quickly as you can.

True tale: What to do with bonuses – a nice worry!

A reader of my *Weekend Herald* column gets regular bonus payments as well as 'a healthy base salary'. She wondered whether to put the bonuses towards reducing her mortgage, paying off her student loan to increase her take-home pay, or investing in share funds.

I told her the rule: Your total wealth is your assets minus your debts. So you can boost your wealth by either reducing your debts or increasing your assets:

- If the debt interest rate is higher than the money you make from an investment, you're better off reducing the debt.
- If the debt interest is lower, you're better off with the investment.

That means paying off the interest-free student loan is not a good idea. But it's trickier to weigh up reducing a mortgage at, say, 5%, with investing in a share fund, because we don't know how well that investment will do.

Chances are good that, over the long term, the share fund will earn more than 5% on average – as explained in Step 4: 'Join the best KiwiSaver fund for you'. But there will be ups and downs that would lead some people to switch to a low-risk fund when the markets fall – and doing that is a great way to destroy wealth.

Because of that, I usually suggest putting most spare money into mortgage repayment, but still investing some into shares and the like so that you spread your risk, and learn about the markets.

> **Moral:** When weighing up repaying debt versus investing, compare the interest you pay on debt with expected investment earnings.

Step 2 check

Have you:

- ❏ Set a goal for paying off your credit card debt?
- ❏ Told friends and family about your goal?
- ❏ Made a diary note when you bought a treat?
- ❏ Started a month's worth of habit changing?
- ❏ Made an appointment for budgeting help (if you need it)?
- ❏ Set yourself up as a credit card winner?

Reward

What did you choose last time? You might want something different this time. A reminder of my suggestions: chocolates, cheese or flowers; or a 'me day' with a walk, book, time with family, being creative; or donating to a charity, or anything else that makes you smile.

What's next? Protecting yourself from falling back into the debt trap.

Step 3

SET UP INSURANCE – AND A RAINY DAY FUND

In which we ...

- Realise why it's good to be ripped off by insurance
- Think about the unthinkable – what would happen if ...
- Learn why it's not just immoral but stupid to lie to an insurance company
- Read about 7 ways to cut insurance costs
- Consider where rainy day money might come from ...
- ... And where you might store it

We've got rid of that hideous high-interest debt – or some of you never had it in the first place (and let's be honest, you read through the last step feeling just a weeny bit smug!).

But as I said, some people got into that pickle because of a financial crisis. So let's set things up so that if you have sudden unexpected expenses – car repairs, dental work, travel for a funeral, money to tide you over after you've lost a job – that doesn't lead to big debt again.

It's quite simple really. Rather than living payday to payday, and hoping all will be well, you have insurance against the big bad stuff, and you also have money readily available – not because you want the latest this or that, but because you need to buy something you can't function without.

Shelter from the storm

Insurance. Sigh! It sounds so boring. But I promise to make it interesting.

For a start, there's nothing boring about coming home to find your home flooded or burnt down or torn apart by an earthquake. Even if you're renting, there's still all your possessions to consider.

And I'll never forget talking to a middle-aged, middle-class mother who had been a homemaker until her husband, an accountant, died suddenly. Despite his career, he had no life insurance. I suppose he just thought there was no way he would die for many years yet.

The woman had to cope not only with grief, and with children devastated by the loss of their father, but also with hurriedly entering the workforce at too low a pay rate.

Insurance matters. And the sad thing is that the people who most need it – those on low incomes with not many resources – are the least likely to have it. Even if you're not well off, please get some basic cover. There are tips below on how to keep the costs down.

But first, let's look at the basic idea. It's best to go through life feeling 'ripped off' by insurance. If you never get your money's worth, that means you haven't had to make many claims.

The people on the other side – those who get back more than they ever paid in premiums (the money you pay for insurance) – are the unlucky ones. They've had lots of bad stuff happen to them, and while their insurance payouts helped, there's still the hassle of claiming and replacing items, and sometimes the heartache of losing a home or a loved one.

It's often said – at least by those in the insurance industry – that New Zealanders have too little insurance. And indeed, we rank pretty low internationally for life and disability insurance, although we're not so bad on contents and cars. We used to be okay on house insurance, too, but some experts are worrying that our homes are now under-insured, since premiums rose a lot in the aftermath of the Christchurch earthquakes.

Some tips on types of insurance

Life insurance

The woman I described above, whose husband died without insurance, probably also didn't have life insurance herself. It's common for non-employed parents not to be insured. But if they die, their partner can struggle with having to pay for child minding, cleaning and all the other tasks homemakers often do.

If you have dependants and you don't want them to feel angry – as well as sad – if you're hit by the proverbial bus, get life insurance. How much? There are several online life insurance calculators. Most are run by insurance companies, so they might be a tiny bit motivated to oversell! But you can rely on the calculator on Consumer NZ's website, www.consumer.org.nz.

(To use it, you have to belong to Consumer NZ. If you don't, I strongly recommend you join. You get unbiased advice on all sorts of products and services – based on trials and research and also surveys of members on things like brand reliability. I never make a major purchase without reading what Consumer says first. And it's great on minor purchases, too. Also, Consumer will go into bat for you if you have a dispute with a company that you can't resolve.)

Choose term life insurance, which covers you for a fixed period – perhaps until your dependent children have flown the coop, or your mortgage is paid off, when you may want to reduce your cover or stop it altogether. On the other hand, don't neglect to add to your life insurance if another child is born or you take on a new mortgage.

You can get much cheaper life insurance that pays out only if you die in an accident. But it's cheap because few people die that way. Don't be sucked in. Your dependants need money regardless of how you die.

Income protection or disability insurance

This is sometimes called loss of income or income replacement insurance. There are various types of policies, some of which come as part of life insurance.

Typically, you will receive money if you are unable to work for a month or three months. The payments may last for a fixed period, or until you're 65.

If you're employed, ask your employer how long they will continue to pay you if you are unable to work. You don't want to pay for cover when your employer will cover you.

Just as with life insurance, non-employed parents also need disability insurance. If a homemaker becomes disabled, extra money would be really helpful.

House and contents insurance

Before non-homeowners skip this bit, it's a really good idea for you to get contents insurance. Bad things are just as likely – if not more so – to happen to your stuff if you are renting.

For homeowners, of course, you need both house and contents covered. How can you tell if, say, a carpet ruined in a flood comes under house or contents? Imagine turning the house upside down and shaking it. What falls is contents. So, with the example of the carpet, it depends on whether it's tacked down or not.

Note that policies vary on whether your damaged items will be replaced with new ones or you'll be given only enough to buy second-hand goods.

It's a good idea to record the serial numbers of all your electronic equipment, to help prove you had it.

Car insurance

You should always get at least third-party insurance, which covers you if you accidentally damage someone else's car. Your vehicle might be an old dunger, but what if you run into a Rolls Royce and it's your fault?

But of course it's better to have cover for your car, too. And be honest when you apply – not just because your mother said you should, but because it could cost you dearly if you're not. It's easy enough to 'forget' when you're applying for car insurance that you've been in a few crashes or committed a couple of serious driving offences. Or you forget to tell the company if you modify the car. Until you claim.

It's much cheaper for the insurance company to check you out only at claim time. Many people never make claims, so the company doesn't ever check them. But when the company comes back after your claim and says, 'Sorry, but you didn't tell us, so you're not covered,' you'll wish you had listened to your mum.

Note that you won't be covered if you're doing something illegal when you crash the car, such as driving drunk. And that's the very time when you're more likely to have an accident. It's simple really – don't drink and drive.

As your car gets older and worth less, keep an eye on the insured value. There's no point in paying to insure a car for $10,000 when it's now worth only $6,000. Or is there?

With my previous car, I had an 'agreed value' – how much the insurance company would pay if the car was written off. Every now and then I would call them and say, 'My car is no longer worth that much. So how much less would the premium be if I dropped the cover?' The reduction in the premium was always so pathetic that I left the agreed value as it was. And when a relative wrote off my car, I was pretty happy to get the higher amount!

However, if your cover is for the 'market value' of your car, the company will pay out only what it's currently worth, so don't pay additional money for insurance above that amount.

True tale: What if the other guy is not insured?

'Something that made a huge difference to us with our car insurance was "cover for uninsured drivers",' says a friend. 'It means if you're in a crash and the other driver is at fault and uninsured, the insurance company will cover your car. It wasn't standard with our third-party insurance, but the salesman suggested it, and it cost something like $3 a year.

'When we had a crash on the motorway, the guy at fault wasn't insured. He had been ordered by the courts to pay us off at about $7 a week. He made two full payments, then half two weeks later, then nothing.

'I had forgotten that I'd got that extra cover. But the company called me up and immediately paid out the full value of our written-off car (no excess), then tried to recover that money from the guy themselves. I was very glad I'd paid that few extra dollars.

'When I got insurance for the next car I had to specifically ask for it, and the salesman hadn't sold it before. But again, it was about $3 a year.'

Moral: Get that extra cover.

Travel insurance

Dispute resolution schemes – which sort out problems between you and financial service providers – say travel insurance problems loom large on their list of disputes. (For more information on dispute resolution schemes, see 'If you have a problem' (page 142), in Step 5: 'Boost your saving painlessly'.)

There are so many things that can go wrong when travelling, and we don't always bother to read all the fine print of insurance that will last for just one holiday.

But it's important to get good travel insurance. There are horror stories of people running up overseas bills of hundreds of thousands of dollars for medical care.

Who to go with – without spending hours researching it for one measly trip? This is the sort of situation when Consumer NZ comes to the fore. Check out their recommendations.

Health insurance

This is a bit like car insurance. It's tempting when applying to 'forget' earlier health problems or pre-existing illnesses. Your premiums will be lower if you don't go into all of that.

Don't be tempted. Again, you won't be challenged until you make a claim. But 'No cover' is the last thing you need to hear when you're unwell.

Some people drop health insurance – perhaps in retirement when the premiums soar – saying the state system will take good care of them. After all, many top medical specialists work in public health as well as privately.

But I don't recommend that. Often health insurance will enable you to get medical attention faster, with more choice about who treats you, and sometimes in a better facility.

When you've got medical problems, these issues – especially the faster service – might matter a lot. Looking at photos of your last holiday, funded by dropping your health insurance, won't quite make up for slower action, less choice and fewer comforts.

Keeping insurance costs down

You can greatly reduce your insurance premiums by skipping cover for the small stuff.

Unless you think you're likely to make more insurance claims than average, it's a good idea to choose high 'excesses' on your car, house and contents insurance. The excess is the amount you yourself pay after a mishap. Let's say you're in a car crash and your excess is $500. You pay the first $500 towards repairs, and insurance covers the rest.

The higher your excess, the less your insurance will cost. Always ask about what excesses are available.

Along similar lines:

- In loss of income insurance, lengthen the period of time you need to be off work before the insurance starts to pay you – perhaps from one month to three months.
- In health insurance, consider dropping cover for GP visits and covering only major medical problems.

The clear downside of this strategy is that when you smash your car, flood your house or visit your doctor, you have to come up with more of your own money. But the savings from lower premiums will probably be worth it, especially if you darken the medical clinic door only occasionally, or claim on insurance less often than average.

I go for high excesses and no GP cover, and when I have to pay I try to remember that not only have I saved lots on premiums, but I don't have to go through the hassle of making an insurance claim for a simple visit to the GP.

Here are some other sources of cheaper insurance and ways to reduce costs:

- Some workplaces offer various insurances for employees, usually at a good rate. It's cheaper for an insurance company to run a program through an employer. Also, as employees tend to be healthier than citizens as a whole, that keeps down costs on things like health and disability insurance.

- You can sometimes reduce your house insurance premiums by installing smoke alarms and burglar alarms, and keeping them in working order. That doubles the advantage of having them – lower insurance costs *and* less bad stuff happening.
- Insurance companies often offer discounts if you place all your insurance – such as car, house and contents – with them.
- Qualify for a no-claims discount on your premiums, by not claiming! The more years you don't need to claim, the larger the bonus. And these are big dollars. On car insurance, after four or five years without a claim your premium might be more than halved. And you won't necessarily lose the discount if you make a claim when another driver was at fault.
- Shop around. Consumer NZ has guidance on which companies to go with. Sometimes there's hundreds of dollars' difference in annual premiums. But take note of different companies' ratings from S&P or AM Best, which Consumer lists. These ratings give you an idea of the companies' financial strength.
- This last point isn't exactly a source of cheap insurance. But as your KiwiSaver balance grows – which I'm sure it will after you've read Step 4: 'Join the best KiwiSaver fund for you' – consider reducing your life insurance. If you die, your dependants can inherit your KiwiSaver money.

True tale: The rip-off man

Years ago, I watched in shock as a man I knew said casually, 'I don't like this suit any more,' and held a cigarette to the trousers so it burnt a hole. He planned to claim 'the accident' on his contents insurance, and get the money to buy a new suit.

Who knows how often that goes on, but it stinks. My so-called friend might have thought he was 'just ripping off the insurance company'. But we all end up paying higher premiums because of insurance fraud.

Of course, insurance fraudsters don't always get away with it. If that guy kept up his antics, one day he might have found that not only was a claim declined and he was left with a ruined suit, but that he was facing criminal charges.

> **Moral:** It's a pretty obvious one – don't be an insurance cheat.

The emergency fund

A rainy day fund and insurance complement one another in a way. The amount you need in your rainy day fund depends to some extent on how much insurance you have – and vice versa. You're covered one way or the other. Some people even call their rainy day fund 'self-insurance'.

Emergency money should be kept slightly out of reach, so you don't dip into it when you feel you've been too stressed lately and you need a weekend away. Do that a few times, and the fund won't be there when you need it.

If you have a credit card, one idea is to put your rainy day money in a one-month term deposit, and keep renewing it. Then use the credit card for the emergency spending. By the time you have to pay the credit card bill, the term deposit will have matured.

Or you could keep the money in one of those bank savings accounts where you lose the higher interest rate if you withdraw money. Most of the time, you won't be withdrawing.

Another option applies if you have an offset, redrawable or revolving credit mortgage. With one of these mortgages, you could use your rainy day money to reduce mortgage interest. (See the heading 'Traditional, offset, redrawable or revolving credit?' (page 252) in Step ?: 'Buy a home, or sell one'.)

True tale: Charity or emergency?

An academic I knew years ago had a great idea for a rainy day fund. At the start of each year he put, say, $1,000 into a bank account and told himself he had given it to charity.

Then if he had unexpected or bad luck expenses at any time during the year, he took the money out of the account. At the end of the year, he gave the remainder to charity.

The charity did well some years, not so well other years, but it averaged out over time. And when bad stuff happened to my friend, he didn't have to pay for it, the charity did!

Moral: Generosity can also help the giver.

How much rainy day money do you need?

If you have too little money in your rainy day fund, you can't cover expenses when you need to. But if you have too much, you're tying up money in a fairly low-interest investment when it could be doing much better elsewhere.

Experts recommend an amount that would cover around

three to six months of household expenses. But it depends very much on your circumstances.

For instance, some people have access to other sources of emergency money:

- If you're paying extra off your mortgage, it's a really good idea to ask the lender if you could borrow that extra back again if you need to. It means you've got a loan at whatever the mortgage interest rate is, which will be well below credit card interest rates. Get the lender's agreement in writing that you can borrow back.
- Even if you haven't been making extra mortgage payments, you may be able to add to your mortgage – especially if you have already paid it down a fair bit. It's worth a try.
- If you're in serious financial trouble, you may be able to withdraw some of your KiwiSaver money. It's not easy. You have to give details of your circumstances, and I'm told that quite a few people are refused. But it's a possibility for the big bad stuff.
- If you suffer serious illness – the language is 'permanent and total disability or near death' – you can take out all your KiwiSaver money. But you have to provide medical evidence.

None of these is an ideal solution, though. You still need a rainy day fund as well.

How do you set up a rainy day fund?

Start small, setting up an automatic transfer of say $20 or $50 a week, on the day after payday or benefit day, into a savings account. Increase that amount – even by as little as $5 a week – every month. Write it in your diary or on the calendar on the fridge door to remind you.

When the total has grown to several hundred dollars, transfer the money to a long-term savings account or bank term deposit.

Don't just settle for whatever your bank offers. After all, this money will be sitting around for years. Check out www. interest.co.nz for the rates offered by different banks. Isn't that being disloyal to your bank? Too often I've seen loyal customers getting worse deals from their bank than new customers. Banks tend to take their long-termers for granted – so why should you look after them?

When – not if, but when – you use your rainy day money

It would be a rare person indeed who gets through life never drawing on their rainy day money. When you do, though, make it a top priority to replenish the fund.

That might be hard if you've been kicked in the financial gut. But please start, even if it's just $5 a week going into a separate account.

The bad times will pass. They almost always do. Your financial wellbeing depends on looking beyond the short term.

Step 3 check

Have you:

- ❏ Insured your life if you have dependants? Very important!
- ❏ Ditto for your income?

- ❏ Checked if you have enough house, contents and car insurance?
- ❏ Considered ways to cut insurance costs?
- ❏ Joined Consumer NZ?
- ❏ Worked out how much rainy day money you need?
- ❏ Set up a rainy day fund?

Reward

Chocolates, cheese or flowers; or a 'me day' with a walk, book, time with family, being creative; or donating to a charity, or anything else that makes you smile.

What's next? It's time to get KiwiSaver doing its best for you.

Step
4

JOIN THE BEST KIWISAVER FUND FOR YOU

In which we ...

- Dismiss the scary worries about KiwiSaver
- Understand why KiwiSaver is so hard to beat
- Learn how even the well off – as well as previous homeowners – can use KiwiSaver to buy a home
- Get a feel for different assets and different types of KiwiSaver funds
- Consider the trade-off between coping with a wobbly balance and having more retirement money
- Work out your type of fund
- See how fees can slash earnings on funds

- Ponder whether high fees are worth it
- Work out which provider is best for you
- Find out if you're on track with your KiwiSaver
- Consider whether you're getting the best out of the scheme
- Look into KiwiSaver for kids

Finally we've got to investing! It was important to get high-interest debt and insurance fixed first, but now we're at the positive stuff, the growth stuff, the 'Hey, look how well I'm doing!' stuff. Yay!

Actually, I hope you're already in KiwiSaver. I wrestled with whether to put the Join KiwiSaver step before the Insurance and Rainy Day Fund step. But I hate the idea of somebody running up further credit card debt because they haven't got an emergency fund, so I had to put that early in the book.

If you are already in KiwiSaver – you've either been automatically enrolled when you got a new job or you've realised what a good deal it is and signed up – that's great. If you're not in, get in!

Anyone who has read my columns, listened to my radio broadcasts or attended my seminars knows that I'm forever urging everyone who can to join KiwiSaver. So are lots of other people in the financial world.

But is the scheme worth the money the government spends on it? Has it really made a big difference to New Zealanders' saving rates? It's hard to tell. Research from some highly respected academics finds that much of the saving within KiwiSaver would have happened anyway.

But I keep hearing from people who say that if it weren't for KiwiSaver they wouldn't have saved anything – or very much.

Despite the research, KiwiSaver seems to have benefited many New Zealanders.

Anyway, this book isn't about government policy. KiwiSaver was started by a Labour government and thrived under a National government. Nobody is suggesting it will ever be phased out, even if governments keep fiddling with it. So let's help you make the most of it – in the best KiwiSaver fund for you. But first, the basics.

Not in KiwiSaver? No excuses!

Since KiwiSaver started in 2007, I've heard plenty of reasons why people haven't joined. Being over 65 used to be a good reason. But if proposed changes go ahead, from 1 July 2019 people of any age will be allowed to join, although those over 65 won't receive tax credits or compulsory employer contributions.

Many other reasons for not joining are just excuses for not getting around to it. This is one situation where laziness *is* actually stupidity (pardon my rudeness!).

Sometimes, though, people are scared they could lose their money in KiwiSaver. 'Look at the finance companies ten years ago,' they'll say. 'My grandma's retirement savings were wiped out.'

My response: KiwiSaver is not the same as the finance companies. Its very structure makes it much safer.

Finance companies took people's money and invested it in ventures that were too risky to be funded by banks, such as unsound property deals run by the finance companies themselves.

On the other hand, KiwiSaver providers – the companies that run KiwiSaver schemes – take your money and invest it in a wide range of term deposits, bonds, shares and so on, issued by entirely separate companies.

The government has made some important changes in recent years.

All KiwiSaver providers have supervisors. A supervisor is a separate firm that watches to see that your money goes where your provider says it's going.

Keeping a close eye on both the providers and the supervisors is the Financial Markets Authority, or FMA. Set up in 2011, the FMA is particularly vigilant around KiwiSaver, mindful that more than half the population is in the scheme. I know that because I've been on the FMA board since it started.

The presence of the FMA doesn't mean things can't go wobbly in KiwiSaver. Indeed, we've already had a few small providers who have called it quits. But their members were transferred to another scheme, with all their savings intact. And anyone who didn't like the new provider was free to move at any time to a different one.

Under the current regulation, the idea that a provider could take off to South America with your money seems ridiculous. There's no government guarantee – at least at the time of writing. But if bad stuff like that did happen, it would be astonishing if the government didn't step in and look after affected KiwiSaver members, guarantee or not.

Look! You probably jump in a car every day or so. Every time, you risk your life or limbs. But, on balance, life is better with cars than without. And you're probably more likely to die or be seriously injured in a car crash than you are to lose money because of a KiwiSaver swindle.

Important note: I'm not saying your KiwiSaver balance won't go down. Unless you're in the lowest-risk type of fund, it will fall sometimes. And the higher the risk level of your fund, the more likely it will fall. But it will go back up again in time. More on that shortly.

> **Key message:** Permanently losing KiwiSaver money from unscrupulous behaviour is extremely unlikely.

What about other reasons for not being in KiwiSaver? Some people really can't afford it – although not nearly as many as say that. If you're on the minimum wage working a 40-hour week, 3% of your pay is less than $20 a week.

One reason that I sometimes hear is: 'I don't know which provider or which fund to join.' Help on that is just around the corner, later in this step.

As for other reasons, I could list them here, and shoot them all down. Let's just say that they're almost never valid.

Why is KiwiSaver so good?

When you're in KiwiSaver, you're investing in a 'managed fund'. (The exception is an offering from Craigs Investment Partners, in which you can choose your own investments including individual shares. But this is suited to more sophisticated investors.)

A managed fund is a pool of money deposited by thousands of people. The managers use that money to buy investments.

Managed funds have been around for decades, and have always been a pretty good alternative to investments like rental property or directly buying your own shares. They're a great way of spreading your money – and therefore spreading your risk – over many different investments. If a few go belly-up, others won't, and you'll be fine.

Sure, you have to pay fees to the fund managers. But they run everything for you – buying and selling investments; gathering in earnings on the money; and enabling you to deposit big or small amounts regularly or whenever you want to.

In non-KiwiSaver managed funds you can often get your money out with perhaps a day or two's notice. Sometimes you can arrange regular withdrawals, which can be particularly helpful in retirement.

Managed funds are perfect for the laid-back investor. I've had my retirement savings in them since the 1970s. Then along came KiwiSaver. It has taken a good type of investment and turbocharged it.

As well as getting interest and other earnings on your money, everyone over 18 and under 65 gets a so-called *tax credit* of 50 cents for every dollar they put in, up to a maximum of $521 a year if you put in $1,043 or more. The KiwiSaver year runs from 1 July through to the following 30 June.

Until 1 July 2019, if you join KiwiSaver after age 60, you get five years of tax credits. So if you sign up at 64, you keep receiving the credits until 69. But while everyone else can withdraw their KiwiSaver money from age 65, you can't until your five years are up.

However, if proposed changes come into effect, the above paragraph will no longer apply from July 2019. Tax credits and the lock-in of savings will stop at 65 regardless of when you join.

Most employees who are contributing 3% or more of their pay also get 3% employer contributions.

Figure 3: Why is KiwiSaver so good? The multiplier

Twice as much in equals twice as much out in retirement

Income	From you (employees: 3% of pay)	From employer (3% taxed)	From government (tax credit)	Total inputs	How much your $$$ is multiplied
$20,000	$600	$495	$300	$1,395	2.33 times
$40,000	$1,200	$990	$521	$2,711	2.26 times
$60,000	$1,800	$1,260	$521	$3,581	1.99 times
$100,000	$3,000	$2,010	$521	$5,531	1.84 times
$200,000	$6,000	$4,020	$521	$10,541	1.76 times
Self-employed	$1,043	zero	$521	$1,564	1.5 times

Figure 3 shows the effect of these two extra inputs.

Let's look first at how Fred fares. He earns $60,000, so his 3% contribution comes to $1,800 a year. His boss puts in $1,260 (that's 3% of Fred's pay, but it's taxed). The government adds the $521 tax credit, so the total going in each year is $3,581. Compare that with Fred's own $1,800 contribution. The total is just under twice as much. And that's powerful.

Let's say that outside KiwiSaver, Fred would have saved $100,000. In KiwiSaver he will have just under $200,000. Wow!

> **Key message:** Twice as much going into savings means twice as big a nest egg at the other end.

For Fred's workmate Millie, a part-timer on $20,000, the deal is even better. If Millie would have saved $100,000 outside KiwiSaver, she'll have 2.33 times that – $233,000 – in the scheme.

What about Katy, who is self-employed? She doesn't get an employer contribution. But still, if she puts in $1,043 a year ($87 a month), the tax credit multiplies her contributions by one and a half. If she would have had $100,000 outside KiwiSaver, she'll have $150,000.

These differences will really affect their retirements – letting them have far better holidays or housing or cars and luxuries than they otherwise could have had.

True tale: KiwiSaver in your sixties

A self-employed couple, both turning 65 soon, asked me how much they should contribute to KiwiSaver to get their maximum tax credit, given it stops when they turn 65.

First I told them the more precise answer: In the year you turn 65 – assuming you've been in KiwiSaver for at least five years – your maximum tax credit is proportionate to how much of the year (ending 30 June) you are under 65.

So if you turn 65 at the end of January, your maximum tax credit is seven-twelfths of $521. To get that you need to deposit seven-twelfths of $1,043, which is $609. You can make the deposit any time in the KiwiSaver July-to-June year, including after your birthday.

Then I told them the easy way: Just put in your usual $1,043. Once you're 65 you can take it right back out again! And in the meantime you should earn a bit of interest on it.

While we're at it, if you are aged between 60 and 65 don't think it's not worth joining KiwiSaver.

As noted above, you can receive tax credits for five years – that's up to $2,605 from the government – as well as earnings on the money. And you can withdraw your deposits plus the tax credits and earnings in five years – although it's often wise not to take out the lot. (More on that in Step 7: 'Head confidently towards retirement – and through it'.)

However, if the proposed July 2019 changes come into effect, tax credits and the lock-in of savings will stop for everyone when they turn 65. That means people aged 60 to 65 should grab the chance to join KiwiSaver before then so you get the five years of tax credits.

Moral: KiwiSaver is not just for the young.

When your employer doesn't really contribute

Some employers – often bigger employers it seems – apply what's called *total remuneration* to KiwiSaver. That means that KiwiSaver members effectively pay their own employer contributions as well as their employee contributions. The employers usually say they do it to prevent employees in KiwiSaver from getting more from the company than people who haven't joined the scheme.

Total remuneration was allowed when KiwiSaver first started, in 2007. It was banned a year later by the Labour government, but allowed again after National won the 2008 election. It has since been criticised by the Commission for Financial Capability, which called it a disincentive to be in KiwiSaver.

At the time of writing (October 2018), the use of total remuneration seems to be on the rise. I wouldn't be surprised if it is banned again – and a good thing, too, in my opinion. I think it's fine to give employees in KiwiSaver an advantage. After all, every New Zealand resident can join.

In the meantime, if you're stuck with total remuneration at your place of work, I urge you to still join and still contribute. You'll get tax credits, and benefit from the growth in your savings.

Of PIES and PIRS – and 'who is my provider?'

There's lots of good news about KiwiSaver and tax. The system is simple, and the tax rates are lower than on most income.

All KiwiSaver funds are what's called *portfolio investment entities* – or PIEs. When you invest in a PIE, the tax on your earnings is lower than on some other investments, such as bank term deposits. For example, the top PIE tax rate is 28%, compared with the top ordinary tax rate of 33%.

Your provider will pay your KiwiSaver tax for you. So you don't need to do anything about it.

But – and this is important – if you haven't told your provider what tax rate you should be on, you will be paying tax at the top rate. If you earned less than $48,000 in both of the past two years, that rate is probably too high for you. It will make a big difference to how fast your KiwiSaver account will grow and how much you'll have at retirement. And you can't get that money back later. It's gone.

The tax rates on PIEs are called *prescribed investor rates*, or PIRs. There are three rates: 10.5%, 17.5% and

28%. To find out which one is right for you, go to www. tinyurl.com/PIRratesNZ.

If you find you should be on 10.5% or 17.5%, you will probably be able to change to that on your provider's website. If not, phone or email your KiwiSaver provider. They should be happy to help you with this. Don't delay. In the meantime, you are being over-taxed!

Don't know who your provider is? You're not alone. A surprisingly large number of New Zealanders who were allocated to what are called default providers when they started a new job have stayed there and taken little interest in finding out more about the scheme.

That's not a good idea. Later in this step I'll show you how to move to the best provider and fund for you. But in the meantime, there's an easy way to find out who your current provider is.

With your IRD number at hand, call Inland Revenue on 0800 KiwiSaver (0800 549 472). They'll tell you your provider, and give you contact details so you can ask the provider which of their funds you are in.

Help to buy a home

Before you flick over this section, thinking it doesn't apply to you, read this: Two large groups of people who can get help with buying a home through KiwiSaver often don't realise it.

The first group is people on high incomes or buying flash houses. Sure, there are income and house price caps if you want to get a grant. But if you don't qualify for that, you can still withdraw your KiwiSaver money to buy a mansion – even if you earn a million dollars a year.

The second group is people who have owned a home in the past but no longer do, and are struggling to get back into the housing market. You may also be able to get help from KiwiSaver.

There's info later in this book (in Step ?: 'Buy a home, or sell one') on how to make the purchase. Here we look only at how KiwiSaver can help you.

First home buyers

There are two parts to KiwiSaver first home help. To qualify for either part, you must intend to live in the house you buy – this is not for rental property.

Part 1: Withdrawing money. After three years in the scheme, everyone – on *any* income – can withdraw everything except $1,000 to use to buy their own first home. The $1,000 stays in your account, with the idea that you will get back into saving for retirement after buying the house. (The $1,000 rule applies regardless of whether you got the $1,000 kick-start when you joined KiwiSaver.) The fact that you can withdraw money contributed by the government and your employer means you'll have lots more than if you had saved for a home outside KiwiSaver.

Part 2: KiwiSaver HomeStart grant. This totals $3,000 after you've been in the scheme for three years, $4,000 after four years, or $5,000 after five or more years. If you and your partner – or anyone else you want to buy a home with – both qualify, you'll get double those amounts. The amounts are also doubled if you buy a newly built home. So a couple can get as much as $20,000, which is a pretty nice gift from the rest of us taxpayers!

To get the grant:

- You must have been regularly contributing to KiwiSaver for at least three years. There are minimum contributions rules, but if you're an employee you will have contributed enough. It's okay if you had a break in contributions, just as long as the contributing periods total three years.
- You need a deposit – including a KiwiSaver withdrawal and the grant – of at least 10% of the price. Mind you, these days you would be lucky to get a mortgage if you didn't have a deposit at least that big anyway.
- Your annual household income can't be more than $85,000 (before tax) for one buyer, and $130,000 for two or more buyers.
- There are maximum house prices. In 2018, the price caps for existing houses were $600,000 in Auckland; $500,000 in Hamilton City, Tauranga City, Western Bay of Plenty District, Kapiti Coast District, Porirua City, Upper Hutt City, Hutt City, Wellington City, Tasman District, Nelson City, Waimakariri District, Christchurch City, Selwyn District, and Queenstown Lakes District; and $400,000 elsewhere in New Zealand.

Add $50,000 to all those prices if you're buying a newly built home.

The income and house price caps are adjusted every now and then, and other conditions of KiwiSaver first home help are sometimes changed. To get updated info, go to www.tinyurl.com/NZFirstHomeHelp.

Previous homeowners

If you no longer own a home, have never used KiwiSaver first home help before, and are not very well off, you may be able to get a HomeStart grant as well as withdrawing your KiwiSaver money.

The idea is that you are in a similar financial situation to first home buyers who can get the grant. You might, for example, have been through a relationship break-up or a bankruptcy or business loss, and have lost your home in the process.

You have to tick all the boxes above: on regular contributions, a deposit, and the income cap and house price cap. And there's one extra hurdle. Your 'realisable assets' have to total less than 20% of the house price cap for existing properties in the area where you plan to buy. The government defines 'realisable assets' as 'belongings that you can sell to help buy a house'.

To work out 20%, divide the price cap by five. For example, if the price cap is $500,000, your realisable assets must total less than $100,000.

Housing New Zealand considers the following to be realisable assets:

- money in bank accounts (including fixed and term deposits)
- shares, stocks and bonds
- investments in banks or financial institutions
- building society shares
- boat or caravan (if the value is over $5,000)
- other vehicles (such as classic motorbikes or cars that you don't use as your usual method of transport)
- other individual assets valued over $5,000
- deposit funds paid to real estate agent

I hope you qualify. This could be a great second start for you.

In KiwiSaver, but not really?

A surprisingly large number – more than one-third – of KiwiSaver members are not contributing. They're on a contributions holiday. (This will be called a savings suspension from 1 April 2019 if proposed changes take effect. Also, the maximum holiday will be reduced from five years to one year.)

I urge you to get back onto the wagon. You may have jumped off because of a short-term cash crunch, or because you're paying off high-interest debt. In fact, I suggested that back in Step 2: 'Kill off high-interest debt'. But hopefully that's past now. And you want to be getting the KiwiSaver incentives along with everyone else.

If contributing 3% of your pay feels just too hard at the moment, put in less. You can do that by sending the money directly to your provider, even if you're an employee. Ask them how. If you put in just $100 a year, you'll get a $50 tax credit. It all helps.

Which fund for you?

Here's a wager. If you're in KiwiSaver, I bet you're not in the best fund for you. I'll lose with a few of you, but not many.

Why aren't you in the best fund? Maybe you don't want to spend time monitoring the different funds, or following the ups and downs of the share market and bond market. You might not even know where to get that info from – or be the least bit interested in it.

The great news is you don't need to do any of that. You can find out the best fund for you in half an hour or so, and then stick with it. As you approach retirement, you might want to make a slight alteration – moving to a lower-risk fund with the same provider. More on that later. But beyond that, your fund choice should be simple, and in most cases done and dusted for a few decades.

How do KiwiSaver funds differ?

We can classify KiwiSaver funds depending on how risky their investments are. But first, let's take a quick look at the different types of investments.

4 types of assets

The four types of assets are: cash, bonds, property and shares.

Cash

This is investments like bank accounts or short-term bank term deposits. They earn interest and never lose their value unless the financial institution defaults. Generally, KiwiSaver managers would invest only in higher quality cash investments, so a default would be unlikely.

Bonds

These are a bit like term deposits. They are issued by central and local governments and banks and other companies. The investor lends money to the government or company issuing the bond for a certain period, say five years. The issuer pays interest and gives back the money at the end of the period – unless they default because they are in financial trouble.

The interest is higher on riskier bonds, simply because the issuer has to pay more or nobody would want their bonds. For example, some local government bonds issued in 2018 paid 2.75%, while some corporate bonds paid 5%.

Again, it's unlikely that many bonds in KiwiSaver funds would default, but it could happen sometimes.

Maths alert! What is a maths alert? I like maths, but I know lots of people aren't so keen. And I don't want you to stop reading because a few numbers have come into play. So I'll make a deal with you:

- Whenever I say 'Maths alert!', I will also explain right afterwards, in words with no numbers, the main point I'm making. So you can skip the numbers if you like.
- But please at least have a quick read through the numbers before you give up. None of the maths is hard. And it will give you a better understanding of what's going on.

Back to bonds. Bonds can be sold before their maturity date. And that leads to another type of risk. Let's say a KiwiSaver fund buys a $1,000 five-year bond that pays 5% interest.

Two years later the fund wants to sell the bond, but in the meantime interest rates have risen and similar bonds are paying 6%. Nobody will be keen to buy the older 5% bond, given they can get 6% on a newer one. So the KiwiSaver fund will have to accept a lower price. The bond might sell for, say, $900.

Whoever buys it from the KiwiSaver fund has got a discount to make up for the lower interest rate, and will still get $1,000 back when the bond matures.

Here's how bond prices work:

- If interest rates have *risen* since a bond was issued, people won't buy the bond unless they get a bargain, below the issue price.
- The reverse also happens. If interest rates have *fallen* since the bond was issued, the bond will be attractive and people will pay extra for it.

You might think that won't affect you in a KiwiSaver fund, as you're not buying and selling. But the fund managers may be trading bonds. And even if they're not, some investors in the fund will be withdrawing to buy a first home or retire. That means the fund managers must keep revaluing their bonds to current market prices, so those withdrawing get a fair price.

Main point (for those who don't like maths): All you really need to know is that bonds can be sold before their maturity date. And interest rates are often on the move – up or down – and so bond values can fluctuate quite a lot. This makes them somewhat riskier than cash.

Property

The property investments in KiwiSaver funds are almost always commercial properties, such as office buildings, factories, and shopping malls. The fund manager will often invest in a property fund that, in turn, owns the buildings. The returns on that fund are made up of rental income plus gains – and minus losses – made when selling the properties.

But – just as with bonds – even when a property fund doesn't sell any properties, it has to take account of any falls in property values. And despite many New Zealanders' eternal optimism about property investments, values do sometimes fall.

KiwiSaver investments in property are, therefore, generally riskier than bond investments.

Shares

These are issued by companies to raise money to grow or run their business. If you buy a share, you own a tiny portion of the company. You'll usually receive regular dividends – your share of the profits – although some rapidly growing businesses keep all their profits to reinvest in their growth.

Share values sometimes fluctuate a lot. If the company does really well, its share price can soar. If it fails, its shares become valueless.

Generally, KiwiSaver managers invest in fairly solid shares, so while the occasional company might fail, the big majority won't. But still, the value of the fund's shares will rise and fall. And, as with the other assets, the fund manager has to include those rises and falls in their fund value.

In the long run, the value of all shares in a market trends upwards, but there can be some big drops on the way. That means shares are, like property, riskier than bonds.

5 types of KiwiSaver funds

Okay, now let's look at the different types of KiwiSaver funds: defensive, conservative, balanced, growth and aggressive. They're classified by their risk level.

When we talk about risk in a KiwiSaver fund, we're not talking about the likelihood that the provider will go belly up. We've already covered that. We're talking here about how volatile a fund is – how many ups and downs it's likely to have.

> **Key message:** Risk in KiwiSaver is not a bad thing. It depends on how much of the fund is invested in growth assets. These are assets that usually grow in value over the long term – shares and property.

Defensive funds

These are the lowest risk. They hold mostly cash and less than 10% in growth assets. Your balance will probably never fall, but it will probably be the slowest growing over the years.

Along with people who really don't want to take any risks with their money, defensive funds suit people who expect to spend their KiwiSaver money within three years – on either a first home or retirement spending. That's because there's too big a chance, over such a short period, that the share or property markets will fall right before you want to spend your money.

Conservative funds

These hold 10% to 35% in growth assets, but mainly they hold cash and bonds. They include *default funds* – the funds that people are put into when they are auto enrolled into KiwiSaver, unless they say they prefer another fund.

If you're in a default fund, you probably won't be by the time you've ended this step! The only situation in which you would stay is if it turns out that a conservative fund suits you best. You might, for example, be uncomfortable with risk or expect to spend the money within two to six years.

Balanced funds

These are the middle level funds, with 35% to 63% in growth assets. That means their values will fluctuate quite a bit. They work well for people who are okay with some wobbles, or who expect to spend the money within about five to 12 years.

Growth funds

Now we're getting to the more exciting stuff. These funds hold 63% to 90% in growth assets, so you've got to be prepared to see your balance fall quite a long way sometimes.

Picture your $50,000 dropping to $30,000! In a growth fund, you must promise yourself that you won't switch to a lower-risk fund when things are bad. Switching like that is a sure-fire way to lose wealth.

You should be expecting to spend the money in ten years or more. That will give your account time to recover from a major downturn before you withdraw the money. But the good news is that over time, growth funds are likely to be the second fastest growing type of fund.

Aggressive funds

These funds are for the brave and the savvy. They hold 90% to 100% in growth assets, and will be volatile. You've got to be totally cool about downturns. In return, you will probably get the biggest long-term growth. And again, the ten-year rule applies. Aggressive funds don't work well for people planning to withdraw their money within less than ten years.

The trade-off

When choosing a type of fund, there's a trade-off. Everything else being equal, pretty much everyone prefers lower risk when it comes to their savings. It might be fun to take a gamble with a Lotto ticket, but it's no fun if you lose big on your long-term money.

But if you go with a lower-risk fund, your average returns over the years will be lower. And that makes a big difference over time.

In our examples in Figure 4, we'll say that the total contributions from all sources into your KiwiSaver fund start at $400 a month. They rise by 2% a year – which is conservative. Since 2000, wages have actually risen by more than 3% a year, but who knows what the future holds?

Figure 4: The higher the risk, the bigger the balance at the end
Total contributions start at $400 a month and rise 2% a year

	Your balance after 10 years	Your balance after 20 years	Your balance after 40 years
Low-risk fund: 1.5% return after fees and tax	$57,000	$135,000	$382,000
Higher-risk fund: 6% return after fees and tax	$72,000	$217,000	$1.045 million

There are two things to notice in Figure 4:

- Return really matters. The difference in balances between the two funds after 10 years is considerable. And after 40 years the higher-risk balance is almost three times as big. The longer the period, the bigger the difference.
- Time also really matters. If you double your time in KiwiSaver – from 10 to 20 years, or from 20 to 40 years – your balance way more than doubles. This is because of compounding returns.

Your contributions might be much lower or higher than $400 a month. If they are closer to, say, $800 a month, double all the numbers in Figure 4. If they are about $200 a month, halve the numbers.

What can we learn from this? It's not a great idea to stay in a low-risk fund, unless you're planning to spend the money within a few years. Sure, you'll have a smoother ride, as our next table, Figure 5, shows. But you'll almost certainly end up with less in your account at the end of the period.

Figure 5 shows:

- There's a bigger chance that your account balance will fall in an aggressive fund than in a lower-risk balanced fund. In the balanced fund, in fact, it's practically impossible for your balance to go down over 10 years. A one in 1,846 chance is minuscule.
- But you can also see that the chance of your balance falling decreases a lot over time. Even in an aggressive fund, over 10 years there's only a slim

Figure 5: Chances of your KiwiSaver account balance falling

The longer the period, the less likely the balance will go down

Investment period	Balanced fund	Aggressive fund
1 year	1 in 7	1 in 4
3 years	1 in 27	1 in 8
5 years	1 in 96	1 in 15
10 years	1 in 1,846	1 in 34

chance your balance will fall. And over longer than 10 years it's even slimmer.

There's another factor here, too. The higher returns on shares and property – the main investments in higher-risk funds – also give you some protection from inflation.

If you look at Figure 12: Different assets take different paths (page 165), you'll see that the shares and property lines have grown much faster than the inflation line. But with bonds, the growth isn't much more than inflation. In Figure 8: Inflation and interest rates (see page 118), you'll see that term deposit returns also tend to stay close to inflation.

Currently, inflation in New Zealand is low – usually between zero and 3%. But back in the 1970s and 1980s it was well above 10%. While it seems unlikely that inflation will get that high again any time soon, there's no guarantee it will stay low. Arguably, then, higher-risk funds, with more shares in them, are in some ways less risky – certainly if inflation gets higher and starts eating into the value of lower-risk funds.

True tale: How we've done
as KiwiSaver turns 10

In mid 2017, to mark the tenth anniversary of KiwiSaver, I asked readers of my *Weekend Herald* column to tell me how well they had done in the scheme.

I confined my survey to people who had made regular contributions and no withdrawals, and asked when they joined, how much they themselves had contributed, and their current balance.

Even though some respondents had been in KiwiSaver for only a few years, most had at least doubled the money they put in – because of government and employer contributions and investment returns. Some had tripled or close to quadrupled their money. Only one particularly unlucky person reported their balance was less than the amount they had put in.

Of course there may be biases in who chose to respond – perhaps towards people who have done well in KiwiSaver, although some took the opportunity to express their disappointment.

It wasn't surprising to see that accounts in higher-risk funds usually performed better. This happens over long periods. But higher risk means higher volatility. The returns of one reader in a growth fund lurched from minus 18% in his first year (during the 2007–08 global financial crisis) to plus 24% in his second year! What a relief he didn't panic after year one and move to a lower-risk fund.

Returns have been particularly good in recent years. The 2007–08 crisis hurt early returns, but people's balances were low then. Since then, markets have been strong. However, some time in the next decade there are sure to be market downturns, which will reduce average returns. And there will probably be some crashes in the years to come. But still, those who keep contributing regardless are sure to end up doing well.

> **Moral:** KiwiSaver is hard to beat if you look at returns on the money you have put in.

Find your type of fund

Hopefully by now you've realised that getting into the most suitable type of fund for you – whether defensive, conservative, balanced, growth or aggressive – is really important. It will almost certainly make much more difference to your final outcome than which provider you go with.

There are lots of online KiwiSaver tools that will help you find your best fund type. The ones I recommend are on www.sorted.org.nz. Sorted is run by the government-funded Commission for Financial Capability (CFFC), so its information is unbiased. The tools are also really helpful and easy to use. (Of course I would say that, because from time to time I've helped the Commission design some online tools!)

The best way to approach the 'Which KiwiSaver fund?' question is to go to the Sorted home page, where you'll find a link to the Get Sorted section. This includes their Step 2: Get your KiwiSaver settings right. That will show you how to find out which type of fund – which risk level – is best for you.

To establish that, you need to answer the following three questions:

- How long before you expect to start spending your KiwiSaver money – for a first home or in retirement?

You get a choice of zero to three years; four to nine years; or ten years or more.

- What's most important to you while you're saving? Getting back at least as much as you put in; almost certainly ending up with more than you put in despite some ups and downs along the way; or getting likely higher returns over the long term, even if that means big ups and downs in some years.
- What range of gains and losses are you comfortable with over a single year? There's a choice of a 0% to 5% gain; a 10% loss to a 20% gain; or a 30% loss to a 100% gain.

As you can see, it's all about two things: your risk tolerance and how soon you expect to spend the money. Sorted processes your replies, and tells you which type of fund is best for you.

Compare all the funds of your type

Once you've established which *type* of fund is best for you, you'll want to find which provider offers the best fund of that type.

While I was writing this book, the Commission for Financial Capability and other agencies were working on a great new online tool for learning more about KiwiSaver and other investments, called Smart Investor. By the time you read this, it should be up and running on www.sorted.org.nz.

Using Smart Investor, you'll be able to sort through funds of the type you're after. You can rank them by:

- how high their fees are; and
- how they've performed on average over the past five years.

Uh oh … I know what you're thinking: 'Why would I bother to look at fees? Performance is all that really matters in the end – how fast my balance will grow.' The trouble is that past returns are old, dead information.

> **Key message:** Past returns don't really tell us anything of value about future returns.

Lots of research shows that funds that have performed well in the past are just as likely – and sometimes more likely – to perform badly in the future. This applies to last month's winners, last year's winners and even last decade's winners. Most of them don't keep doing well in the following month, year or decade.

More on this in Step 6: 'Stay cool', but for the moment take my word for it – info on past performance is pretty much useless for predicting future returns.

However, there are two uses for data about past returns.

The first is that you might want to avoid a fund that has consistently performed much worse than other similar funds. Maybe it's just badly managed.

The second is that a quick glance at a fund's yearly returns on Smart Investor will show you the *range* of recent returns. Here's what you're likely to see:

- In a low-risk fund, the returns year after year will almost always be positive but low.
- In a middle-risk fund, they will occasionally be negative, and might range up to 10%, sometimes more.
- In a high-risk fund, they're more likely to be negative every now and then – be prepared for rare drops of more than 25% – and might range up to 25% or more.

This gives you a feel for the range you might expect in the future. But don't dwell on returns. Instead, concentrate on which funds have the lowest fees.

> **Key message:** Rank the funds according to their fees first, and put most weight on this.

Fees are the charges that providers regularly take out of your account to cover their costs and give them a profit. They are the main thing to consider when choosing a provider. This is such an important message that I'm going to take a few pages to – I hope – convince you.

How fees can slash returns

The lower the fees, the more likely after-fees returns will be higher.

Figure 6 shows what a *huge* difference fees make to how fast your savings grow. And the longer you're in KiwiSaver, the bigger the difference.

If you're in a higher-risk fund for 40 years, you'll have more than $200,000 extra in retirement if you go for the lowest fees instead of the highest fees. That's serious money. (And, by the way, the numbers are for someone who is taxed at the top PIR rate. If your rate is lower, the numbers would be even higher.)

The fees used here – written underneath each table – were the lowest and highest actually charged by KiwiSaver funds in March 2018. It's an astonishingly wide range, with the highest fee being at least three times the lowest.

Figure 6: High fees can clobber your KiwiSaver account

Total contributions from all sources start at $250 a month and rise 2% a year

Low-risk fund

After 20 years: your balance with lowest fee	After 20 years: your balance with highest fee	After 40 years: your balance with lowest fee	After 40 years: your balance with highest fee
$85,000	$80,000	$245,000	$214,000

Return after tax and before fees: 2% a year.
Lowest fee: 0.47%. Highest fee: 1.48%.

Medium-risk fund

After 20 years: your balance with lowest fee	After 20 years: your balance with highest fee	After 40 years: your balance with lowest fee	After 40 years: your balance with highest fee
$104,000	$95,000	$366,000	$302,000

Return after tax and before fees: 4% a year.
Lowest fee: 0.53%. Highest fee: 1.74%.

Higher-risk fund

After 20 years: your balance with lowest fee	After 20 years: your balance with highest fee	After 40 years: your balance with lowest fee	After 40 years: your balance with highest fee
$139,000	$117,000	$684,000	$474,000

Return after tax and before fees: 7% a year.
Lowest fee: 0.80%. Highest fee: 2.88%.

But wouldn't a fund with high fees be better?

If I pay more for something I usually get better quality. Don't high fees mean higher returns?

In short, no. Lots of research – including by New Zealand's Financial Markets Authority – shows high fees and high returns don't necessarily go together.

Generally speaking, high-fee funds probably do about as well, on average, as low-fee ones – *before we subtract the fees*. After we've done that, the low-fee funds tend to do better on average.

This is controversial stuff. Many KiwiSaver providers who charge high fees say their funds perform better. When I've looked more closely at how some providers come up with these claims, their research can be challenged. But even where it holds up, the question remains: will they keep doing better in future?

The high-fee providers' argument goes something like this: With the bigger fee income, they can pay high-salaried experts to do lots of research and choose which shares or bonds to buy and sell, and when to buy and sell them.

Their funds are called 'active' funds – as opposed to 'passive' or 'index funds', which don't have any investment experts. Index fund managers simply invest in all the shares – or bonds or other investments – in a market index.

What is a market index?

Most market indexes cover the share market. Examples are the NZX50, which includes the biggest 50 shares traded in New Zealand, or the Dow Jones Industrial Index, which includes some of the largest US companies.

You've probably heard in the financial news that the NZX50 has risen 8 points today, or fallen 5 points. The people – or rather the computers – putting the index together take into account the price changes of the biggest 50 shares and calculate the index change. It's a sort of average of how all the shares have done. Broadly speaking, it shows you how the market has performed.

I suggest you don't take much notice of daily market changes. (More about that in Step 6: 'Stay cool'.) But indexes are useful for showing us long-term market trends. They're also used by index funds.

The managers of index funds have an easy ride. They don't need to think about what to invest in and when. They change their investments only when their index changes, which is not often.

With no research to fund, index funds can charge much lower fees. But you would think the lack of research would leave them with lower returns, wouldn't you?

The share market is a funny place. It's all about the future. Every investor wants to know which share prices are going to rise, so they can buy those shares now and sell later at a gain.

For the experts, who are investing not just their own money but many other people's savings, that means watching companies closely for signs of good news about their future – or bad news, in which case they will sell.

Let's say a company announces that it has signed a big contract that will double its sales next year. Or the company appoints a new boss who has performed really well in her last three positions. Lots of people will want to buy shares in that company. And whenever lots of people want to buy anything – whether it be apples, used cars or shares – sellers ask for higher prices.

The trick is to get in and buy shares before the price rises. The trouble is, it will rise fast. It's only really the first one or two people who get in at the beginning who get a good low price. Then the news spreads fast, and other buyers pay 'market price', which is already higher.

If an active fund manager could always – or even often – be the first one to spot the good news about many different companies' futures, their fund would undoubtedly do well.

But there are many other active fund managers trying to get in first. After several decades of reading the research and watching the markets, I don't have any faith that any single manager will buy first often enough for their fund to continually be an outstanding performer.

The same goes for selling. Everyone wants to be first to hear the bad news, so they can sell before the price falls. But only the first one wins. By the time the rest of the active managers sell, they get a low price.

What if I'm wrong? What if one fund manager really *can* often get in first?

There are a couple of reasons why a particularly successful active fund is unlikely to stay successful:

- *The star stock picker leaves.* Even if one expert really was able to pick shares better than anyone else, is she or he likely to stay with the same fund manager? Such a talent would be much in demand, and likely to be enticed away by other fund managers' huge salary offers. Meanwhile, you are sitting in his or her former fund, oblivious to the fact that the genius has gone – although history has shown that such geniuses often fall flat on their faces a little way down the track anyway.

- *Some funds become too big for their boots.* If an active fund has done well lately it will attract more and more investors. As the fund size grows, it's harder for it to trade without its size affecting prices, especially in the small New Zealand market. For example, if the managers want 3% of the fund to be invested in a share, they will go into the market to buy. But the fund has to buy so many shares that, by the time it has bought just a portion, its own purchases will have pushed up the price.

> **Key message:** Investing in an active fund because it's done well lately is not a good idea.

But don't listen to me, listen to American Warren Buffett – one of the world's richest people. He made his money by investing in shares – not in the way most active managers do, but by carefully selecting companies and sticking with his investments, often for decades.

Said Buffett in the 2017 annual report of his company, Berkshire Hathaway: 'Performance comes, performance goes. Fees never falter ... When trillions of dollars are managed by Wall Streeters charging high fees, it will usually be the managers who reap outsized profits, not the clients. Both large and small investors should stick with low-cost index funds.'

You might want to listen to a really good 10-minute BBC podcast on index funds at www.tinyurl.com/BBCindex.

If you prefer the story with pictures, see 'How to Win the Loser's Game' on www.youtube.com. Part 1 runs for six minutes, or you can watch the full version, which runs for one hour and 21 minutes – all pretty interesting.

What do the critics of index funds say? Some say index funds don't perform as well in downturns, when active funds will beat them.

Research findings on this vary. But even if index funds don't do as well when markets are falling, most of the time – and over the long term all the time – markets rise. Given that nobody is good at predicting downturns, get into index funds and stick with them through thick and thin – with your KiwiSaver money and other long-term savings.

You'll be in good company. In recent years, there has been a huge swing, around the world, towards index funds.

Enough on this. It's a hobby horse of mine and it's time I dismounted. I'll just add that I've been watching the active versus index fund debate since about 1980, when I first invested in index funds in the US, where I lived at the time. And I've never looked back.

How to identify an index (or passive) fund

Look for the words 'index' or 'passive' or 'tracker' in their name. Or, more simply, just look at the fees. If they're really low, it's highly likely to be an index fund.

For KiwiSaver funds, you can check the fees in Smart Investor.

Two KiwiSaver brands that are largely passive are Simplicity and SuperLife. ASB and Lifestages also have many passive funds, and Booster and AMP have some.

Smartshares, which is owned by NZX (the company that runs the NZ stock exchange), offers non-KiwiSaver passive 'exchange traded funds', or ETFs. You invest in an ETF in the same way as you would in a share listed on the stock exchange. But instead of buying into a company, you have bought into a share fund. Once you've bought your ETF shares, they function pretty much the same way as an investment in a non-listed managed fund, such as a KiwiSaver fund.

Another option is to invest in the huge US passive investing firm Vanguard, perhaps by opening an account with New Zealand-based InvestNow. The fees are really low, but it's a bit more complicated to invest in an overseas vehicle like this, so it may not be your cup of tea.

Who won in Oz? And how does NZ look?

Here's a couple of examples of research on active versus index funds.

First, Australia. S&P Dow Jones looked at the performance of Australian active funds. Firstly, they made a list of the funds that had done well – the ones in the top quarter of the class – in the five years ending December 2011. How did they do in the following five years, ending December 2016?

Nearly 20% stayed in the top quarter. If you had invested in one of those funds, you would be pretty happy. But a bigger group – more than 23% – didn't just slip into mediocrity; they ended up in the bottom quarter. How would you have felt if you had backed one of those?

The results were even more dramatic when they looked at the funds in the top quarter in a single year, 2012. Only a tiny 2.2% stayed in the top quarter in 2013 through 2016. The performance of all the rest was mediocre or bad. And investors paid relatively high fees for that.

This swinging from doing really well to doing really badly isn't uncommon for active funds. The managers who do well are often those who take a punt or two. They're bigger risk takers. Sometimes this pays off brilliantly, but sometimes it bombs.

What about New Zealand? I haven't seen similar studies done here. But independent research at AUT's Auckland Centre for Financial Research on returns on New Zealand managed funds 'suggests that no fund outperforms over the long term'.

Said AUT lecturer Ayesha Scott, 'Overwhelmingly all the research in this area continues to come back to point out that active managers cannot consistently outperform an appropriate benchmark. That has been shown again and again.'

There's an interesting online tool put together by the Financial Markets Authority called the KiwiSaver Tracker. You can find it at www.tinyurl.com/KSTracker. It's a complicated looking creature, but if you're in a mood to explore you can learn some interesting stuff.

For one thing, you can see how fees impact on returns in each KiwiSaver fund. And if you click on 'Dig into the data' at the top, up will come a graph showing the relationship between KiwiSaver funds' fees and after-fee returns over the past five years.

To get a better idea of what's going on, click on the different types of funds – defensive, conservative and so on.

If higher fees gave us higher returns, the dots on the graph would slope from the bottom left (low fees and low returns) to the top right (high fees and high returns). But they don't.

The numbers are updated every quarter, so by the time you look at this they will have changed. But I would be very surprised if the graphs don't continue to show dots all over the place. Some high-fee funds have high returns, but some have low returns. Ditto for low-fee funds.

It's particularly interesting to look at aggressive funds. Most of these hold nearly all shares, so arguably they are the ones where active high-fee management would make the biggest difference. But if anything, the graph over different periods has tended to show that low-fee funds have performed better.

One thing that worries me about the KiwiSaver Tracker is that you might end up dwelling on which funds have performed well in the past. Please note what's written in red: 'Past returns are no guarantee of future performance.'

Finally! Choosing the fund for you

There are two variations on the KiwiSaver theme that you might want to consider.

First variation: ethical or socially responsible funds

There's a growing tendency for people to take an interest in the types of companies their KiwiSaver fund invests in. You might not want manufacturers of arms, cigarettes, alcohol, gambling products and so on. Or you might want companies with clean green strategies, or good employment practices, or all of the above.

In response, providers are offering more choices in what are called ethical or socially responsible funds. There are varying claims made on whether these funds provide higher or lower returns than other funds. Suffice to say the returns are probably at least as good, so you can go ahead and invest ethically without sacrificing returns.

Many KiwiSaver providers say they filter out investments that might be considered unethical, such as tobacco or weapons. There are also the following specifically ethical funds:

- Balanced funds: AMP Responsible Investment Balanced Fund, Booster Socially Responsible Investment Balanced Fund, Craigs Investment Partners Quaystreet Balanced SRI Fund, and Superlife Ethica Fund;
- Growth funds: Booster Socially Responsible Investment Growth Fund;
- Aggressive funds: ANZ Sustainable International Share Fund.

Note that there are no lower-risk funds. If you prefer lower risk, I wouldn't recommend investing in an ethical fund – unless a new one comes up that is low risk. You don't want to be righteous but worried about volatility!

For more about how these funds invest – and about other new funds that might also be ethical – see their providers' websites. If you choose one of these funds, I still suggest you go for one with low fees.

Second variation: set and forget

If you don't want to have to remember to move your KiwiSaver money to a lower-risk fund as you approach retirement, you might like to use a 'life stages' fund. Several providers offer them.

These funds automatically put young people, with many years before retirement, into higher-risk funds and then reduce the risk as they get older, without them doing anything. These funds are hassle-free, but there are a few possible downsides:

- They don't work well for younger people who are expecting to spend some of their KiwiSaver money on buying a first home within the next ten years. They shouldn't be in a higher-risk fund.
- Other young people – those who already own a home or don't plan to buy one – might not cope with the volatility of a riskier fund.
- Sometimes people nearing 65 are put in a low-risk fund when they don't plan to spend their KiwiSaver money for a decade or more, so would be better off in something riskier.

Still, the idea might work well for you. The following are KiwiSaver life stages funds or similar: AMP Lifesteps Investment; ANZ Lifetimes; Aon LifePoints Target Date funds; Fisher Funds GlidePath; Generate Stepping Stones; Lifestages Age Auto; NZ Funds LifeCycle; OneAnswer Lifetimes; SuperLife Age Steps. Again, watch the fees when making your selection.

4 steps to selecting your best fund

If neither ethical nor set-and-forget funds particularly appeal to you, then here are the steps to take:

1. You're already worked out which type of fund is best for you – defensive, conservative, balanced, growth or aggressive. Go to Smart Investor, and within your type of fund, list the five funds with the lowest fees.
2. Delete any with returns over several years that are way below average.
3. Look at each provider's website, to see if you like the feel of it and what they offer.
4. Read details about the finalists on Sorted.

The Sorted information on each fund includes a short description of the fund from the provider, which will include info on ethical investing if that applies. There's also a breakdown of the types of investments in the fund – what proportion is in cash, bonds, property, shares and other investments.

Note that in this section you can get an idea of how much of the fund's investments are based outside New Zealand. If you're in a lower-risk fund it will probably be quite low. But higher-risk funds often have a large proportion of overseas investments – and that's good. So, if you're struggling to decide between a couple of funds, go with the one with more offshore investments. (There's more on why overseas investments are good in Step 5: 'Boost your saving painlessly'.)

You'll also see a list of the fund's individual investments. You will probably see some familiar names there – of banks, companies and so on. And you'll find a list of key personnel. This probably won't mean a lot to you, but you can always Google the names and learn more about the people if you're curious.

How did that go? *Have you zeroed in on one best fund for you?* If you can't decide between two or three finalists, please don't do what most of us tend to do in those situations – put it all aside to think about it overnight. That's because overnight tends to become overweek, overmonth and overyear. Before you know it, you've missed out on getting the best out of KiwiSaver for an appreciable amount of time. If there really are a few funds that look equally good, close your eyes and point to one. It probably won't make much difference which one you go with.

Chances are high that your new best fund (as opposed to new best friend!) is with a provider that's new to you. Don't worry if you've never heard of them. As I said before, KiwiSaver providers are closely monitored, and some of the less-known providers are, in my opinion, amongst the best ones.

Switching providers should be easy. Just ask the new provider – via their website or by phone – for a form. They will take care of telling Inland Revenue and arranging for your money to be transferred. It may be done within a week, and is usually done within a month.

A few providers charge a small transfer fee if you move out of their scheme. Their argument is 'why should other members subsidise the cost of your move?', which seems fair enough. Anyway, the transfer fees are small enough – often around $30 – not to make any difference in the long run.

Some less than clever reasons for switching KiwiSaver provider

- The provider has had great returns recently. I hope you've got the message by now – good past returns usually don't continue.
- You're trying to get a mortgage, and the bank implies it will look more kindly upon you if you have your KiwiSaver account with them. If you feel you must move for this reason, move back to the best provider for you after you have secured the mortgage.
- You like bank providers because when you log into your bank account online, you can see your KiwiSaver balance. This reasoning scares me! It's fine when the markets are doing well and account balances are growing – as they have done over most of the life of KiwiSaver. But there will – not might, but will – be times when balances fall quite fast. That's when you

must stick with your investment. More on that later. But seeing your balance daily will surely make that harder. I absolutely don't recommend following your KiwiSaver progress that closely.

- Someone you know says they have done really well in their KiwiSaver fund. In the past few years, the markets have performed exceptionally well, with few downturns, and pretty much all funds have done well. Some people are more easily impressed than others!

Are you on track with your KiwiSaver savings?

From May 2019, you should be able to get some idea of this from your KiwiSaver annual statement, which your provider has to send to you around May each year. The statement will include an estimate of how much you will have in KiwiSaver when you retire, and how much you will have available to spend each year in retirement.

That worries me a bit, though. To come up with those numbers, the providers will have to make lots of assumptions.

To get a better idea of what's going on, go through the following little exercise. The first thing you need to ask yourself is: 'How much do I want to spend in retirement – over and above NZ Super?'

In 2018–19, NZ Super for a single person living alone is $463 a week, or about $24,000 a year, before tax. For a married couple with both qualifying, it's $702 a week, or about $36,500 a year.

We don't know how that might change. But if you're older than 40ish, it's probably safe to assume it will be about the same as now in terms of what you can buy with the money. If you're younger, it might be a bit lower – but I doubt if hugely lower. (More on this in Step 7: 'Head confidently towards retirement – and through it'.)

Let's say you would like to spend $200 a week above NZ Super. Go to the KiwiSaver Savings Calculator at www.sorted.org.nz, which will give you a rough estimate of your KiwiSaver balance at 65, and how much you can spend per week in retirement.

If it's less than the $200 you would like to have available, there are two steps you can take:

- Make extra contributions to KiwiSaver. On the calculator you can increase your work contributions, or add extra one-off or regular payments. Make adjustments until you get to $200 a week.
- Reduce the age you enter for life expectancy – from the average of 91 for males or 94 for females.

I'm not suggesting you plan to pop off younger! But the calculator is actually looking at when you'll use up your KiwiSaver money, rather than when you die.

Many people say NZ Super is enough once you're in your mid eighties. (If it's not, there are suggestions on what to do in Step 7: 'Head confidently towards retirement – and through it'.) So switching your 'life expectancy' to, say, 85, is not unreasonable.

The calculator's results are adjusted for 2% inflation. If it says your balance at 65 is $300,000, that means your savings will buy the same as $300,000 buys today. You can switch off the inflation adjustment if you prefer. There are some other important points about this calculator. For details, click on

'How this tool works'. But the main points are that it assumes the following:

- If you're employed, your pay will rise by 3.5% a year, so your contributions will rise to match. That might seem too high; pay rises these days are rarely that big. But in the course of a lifetime, most people get a big pay rise every now and then when they move jobs, and that pushes up your average annual rise. If you're not an employee, it assumes your contributions will increase with inflation – a dodgy assumption given that many non-employees have always contributed $1,043 a year to maximise their tax credit. But I suppose the government will sometimes increase the tax credit – and non-employees will then raise their contributions.
- You take no contributions holidays and make no first home withdrawal.
- You will retire at 65. If you retire at, say, 67, you'll have quite a lot more savings. That's because your balance at 65 is big, so even a 3% return on that money amounts to a lot. For example, if you would have $500,000 at 65 but you retire at 67, you'll have more than $30,000 extra.
- You invest in a balanced KiwiSaver fund. That means your annual return, after tax and inflation, ranges from 2.4% to 3.3% depending on your tax rate. But if you are in a defensive, conservative or default fund, your balance at retirement will probably be lower than the calculator says. And if you're in a growth or aggressive fund, your balance will probably be higher.

To check your results in a lower- or higher-risk fund, access Sorted's KiwiSaver chatbot on Facebook. Just look up Hey Sorted.

Of course, retirement saving isn't only about KiwiSaver. For a more comprehensive look at your situation, use the Retirement Planner on Sorted. (And there's lots more in Step 7: 'Head confidently towards retirement – and through it'.)

Getting the best out of KiwiSaver

Pick the situations that apply to you.

Should you contribute to KiwiSaver or pay down high-interest debt?

While it seems a pity to be missing out on the KiwiSaver incentives, you'll actually be improving your wealth more by paying off credit card and other debt (as explained in Step 2: 'Kill off high-interest debt'). But pay off the debt as fast as possible, so you can get back on the KiwiSaver wagon.

Should you contribute to KiwiSaver or pay extra off a mortgage?

Contributing to KiwiSaver is generally wiser than paying extra off a mortgage, because of the KiwiSaver incentives.

Having said that, if you have a mortgage and you're an employee, put only 3% of your pay into KiwiSaver, as that will still get you the maximum employer contributions and the maximum tax credit. If you can save more than 3% – and I hope you can – put the rest into speeding up your mortgage payments.

Quite a few employees regularly contribute more than 3% of their pay. If that's you, and you have a mortgage, just ask your employer to reduce your percentage to 3%. (The one exception to this is people earning less than $35,000; see next heading.)

For non-employees with a mortgage, contribute $87 a month or $1,043 a year. Put the rest into getting rid of that home loan.

Who should contribute extra to KiwiSaver?

Anyone can put any extra savings into KiwiSaver whenever they want to, by sending it to their provider. Call or email and ask them how to do it. It should be easy.

However, generally I'm not all that keen on people putting extra into KiwiSaver – for the sole reason that it's hard to get the money out again if you need it.

Sure, you can access some or all of your savings if you are seriously ill or in dire financial straits. But it's not easy to do that – especially in the latter situation. And in any case, you might want to access your savings in other circumstances. What say you or a family member wants to start a business? Or a relative needs support?

For most people it's best to have some non-KiwiSaver money saved up elsewhere. For more on that, see the next step.

However, there are three groups of people who should try to contribute extra to KiwiSaver: those on low incomes; big spenders; and the 'keep it simple' crowd.

Those on low incomes. If you make less than $35,000 a year, and you're contributing 3% of your pay, your contributions will total less than $1,043 a year. That means you're not getting the maximum tax credit. So try to get your contributions up to that level.

Here's how. In early June, find out how much you have contributed since 1 July in the previous year. You might be able to work it out from your payslips. It doesn't have to be down to the last cent. A rough count will do. Or call or email your provider. If they're good, they might have written to you about this anyway.

Let's say your total is $800. To get to $1,043, you need to put in an extra $243 – directly to your provider – before 30 June.

Big spenders. If you're the type to raid your long-term savings to buy something, it might be best if you park the savings in KiwiSaver so you can't get your sticky fingers on it.

The 'keep it simple' crowd. Many people prefer to keep their finances simple. If you don't want to have another long-term savings account as well as KiwiSaver, that's fair enough. Just be aware that you're tying up the money and limiting your options.

Nervous but feeling adventurous?

Most people have their money in just one KiwiSaver fund. But, while you're not allowed to be with more than one KiwiSaver provider, you can invest in more than one fund with the same provider.

Why would you want to? Let's say you've noted that if you take higher risk you're likely to have higher returns. But the idea of seeing your balance fall a long way in a riskier fund scares you.

You could start out by putting, say, a quarter of your KiwiSaver money into a higher-risk fund, and leaving the rest in a middle- to low-risk fund. Your provider should help you set this up. See how you cope, over several years, with the volatility in the higher-risk fund. If you don't panic, gradually move more of your money into that fund.

KiwiSaver for kids

There are some different rules for under-18 KiwiSavers:

- They get no tax credits.
- They are not auto-enrolled in KiwiSaver if they start a job.
- But if they are already in the scheme – perhaps enrolled by their parents – 3% will be deducted from their pay and put into KiwiSaver unless they are on a contributions holiday.
- Their employers don't have to contribute to their accounts, although some do.

There used to be a $1,000 kick-start for KiwiSaver, including for children. If the government brings it back, I would certainly recommend you sign up your child to get that money.

Even if that doesn't happen, I think it's best to get them into the scheme. They will start contributing when they get a job, and that can set them up as savers for life. The ones who start young are the ones who will retire with big bucks.

But don't talk to them about retirement. That's too distant for the young. They can't imagine ever being that old! They can, though, focus on buying a first home with KiwiSaver help.

Should parents contribute regularly to their child's account? Maybe not, as the money is then tied up for a first home or retirement. You might want to instead save elsewhere for them, so your child can use the money for tertiary education or starting a business.

But once the 'child' turns 18, it all changes. They are now eligible for tax credits, and it's a pity if they miss out. So if they are studying or aren't able to put much of their own money into KiwiSaver, you might want to put up to $1,043 a year into their account so they benefit from the tax credit. An easy way to do that is via a bank transfer of $87 a month. If – looking forward – you think that will be difficult for you to afford, consider saving up for it when the kids are younger.

And, by the way, this isn't confined to parents. Grandparents, aunties and uncles and others might want to set this up. It's a great way to give a young person a good start – subsidised by the government!

Great-grandpa's gift

An elderly man asked me about putting $30,000 into each of his great-grandchildren's KiwiSaver accounts. 'Would they be able to use the money when applying for a first home grant?' he asked.

Yes, I replied, if they're eligible for a grant. But even if they're not eligible – because their income or house price is too high – they could still withdraw the money to put towards a first home.

Depositing the money into KiwiSaver is a good way to ensure it goes into a property, as opposed to being squandered on cars, entertainment or other stuff. It's hard to predict what the young might get up to!

But I have two slight reservations:

- Some of the young ones may not want to ever buy a home, preferring to rent all their lives. (More on that in Step ?: 'Buy a home, or sell one'.) But that's no big deal, as they would then need to retire with more money, and the $30,000 compounding over the years would be a big boost to their KiwiSaver retirement sum.
- Don't forget to provide for any further great-grandkids. You might even set something up to cover children born after you die. A $30,000 gift is sizable, and offspring who miss out might feel hard done by.

> **Moral:** Use KiwiSaver to steer your support for the young ones in the first home direction.

Don't delay joining

If you've read all the way through this step and you *still* haven't joined KiwiSaver, I hope Figure 7 will convince you.

Remember our young twins, Sally and Suzy, in Step 1: 'Start now – it's easy'. Sally joins KiwiSaver now, but Suzy delays for three years and ends up with $100,000 less. The 'Start now!' message really applies to KiwiSaver. Every year you're out of the scheme is another year you miss out on the turbocharging.

Figure 7 shows some more examples, for people of different ages.

Figure 7 shows that if an employee joins KiwiSaver at 22, she will have $65,000 more at retirement than if she mucked around for two years and joined at 24. For a 42-year-old, delaying isn't quite so damaging, but still he'll miss out on $20,000 in retirement.

Figure 7: Two years matters in KiwiSaver

Savings for employee in balanced fund who earn $35,000 a year at the start

Age	Savings at 65 if you join now	Savings at 65 if you join in 2 years	Difference
22	$538,000	$473,000	$65,000
32	$275,000	$239,000	$36,000
42	$128,000	$108,000	$20,000

Source: KiwiSaver Savings Calculator on www.sorted.org.nz

We should note that the $65,000, $36,000 and $20,000 are not adjusted for inflation. So the amounts won't mean as much then as they do nowadays. But still, I'm sure our 22-, 32- and 42-year-olds will find some fun stuff to do with that money.

And by the way, we're assuming they invest in balanced funds. If instead they choose higher-risk funds, all the totals will be higher.

Step 4 check

Have you:

- ❏ Joined KiwiSaver?
- ❏ Checked that you're not paying too much tax?
- ❏ Got off that contributions holiday?
- ❏ Decided which type of fund is best for you?
- ❏ Decided which provider is best for you?
- ❏ Switched to the best fund and provider?
- ❏ Checked whether you're on track?
- ❏ Made changes so you get the best out of the scheme?

Reward

Chocolates, cheese or flowers; or a 'me day' with a walk, book, time with family, being creative; or donating to a charity, or anything else that makes you smile.

What's next? There's more to saving than just KiwiSaver.

Step 5

BOOST YOUR SAVING PAINLESSLY – HOW AND WHERE

In which we ...

- Learn saving tricks
- Admire some super-savers and worry about over-savers
- Find out why today's interest rates aren't so pathetic
- Learn a quick way to tell how well your property has grown
- Head overseas with your savings

- Understand why individual shares are not great for most of us
- Contemplate a landlord's nightmare
- Know where to go if you're hard done by
- Become aware of all the scammers' tricks

We've got your KiwiSaver set up and working brilliantly. Now it's time to save more. If you're one of the ones who's better off doing that in KiwiSaver – you're on a low income or you're a big spender or you like to keep things simple – that's fine. If not, we'll look at other options in a minute.

But first, for everyone: how do you boost your saving rate?

Hot tips on how to become a big saver

Open a separate savings account in your bank. If they have an interest-earning account in which you pay penalties if you make too many withdrawals, that's even better. Then:

- Set yourself a goal. See 'A quick reminder', below.
- Pay yourself first. Set up an automatic transfer into the account every payday – or every week or month if you don't get regular income. Then think in terms of spending what you haven't saved, rather than saving what you haven't spent.
- Start small, with maybe as little as $10 or $20. Gradually increase it – perhaps by $10 on the first of every month.
- Play mind games. Imagine you've lost your job and your new job pays 5% less. You would manage because you would have to. So increase the automatic transfer by 5% of your pay.

- If your expenses decrease – perhaps you've just paid off a loan, or quit smoking (well done!), or you discover a cheaper electricity company, or a child leaves home – boost your savings by half the extra money. (This is a one-way street. When your expenses rise, don't reduce your savings. Live with it!)
- If the government cuts taxes, save the extra take-home pay, or at least part of it.
- If you receive a one-off payment – an inheritance or a win – celebrate with a small portion but use the rest to really boost your savings.
- Find a picture that symbolises what you're saving for. Perhaps it's the Eiffel Tower in Paris, or a back in a beautiful bay. Put the picture where you'll notice it often.
- Promise yourself that every time you get a pay rise – in your current job or when you start a new job – you'll add half the extra money to your regular savings.

The last item is based on the research of University of Chicago Nobel Laureate Richard Thaler. He's a great thinker about how real people live, and he says many of us find it hard to increase our savings out of our current income.

It's easier to deny yourself in the future than now, says Thaler. 'For example, given the option of going on a diet three months from now, many people will agree. But tonight at dinner, that dessert looks pretty good.'

But if you promise yourself to 'save more tomorrow', it works. Design your own scheme – which could apply to a decrease in expenses or a tax cut as well as a pay rise – and stick to it.

A quick reminder

Remember back in Step 2: 'Kill off high-interest debt' we talked about setting a goal to get rid of debt? The same tips apply to setting a savings goal.

Goals that work are SMART: specific, measurable, achievable, (w)ritten and time-bound.

It's a great idea to promise yourself to save a certain amount by the end of the year, and perhaps another much larger amount ten years from now. Give yourself small rewards when you reach milestones towards your goal.

Champion savers

I'm hesitating to write this. A while back I ran a reader's letter in my *Weekend Herald* Q&A column from a woman who had managed to save up to buy a house on an income of $30,000 a year.

In the following week, two readers wrote angry letters to me. One ran along the lines of: 'It's all very well for some people, but we're trying to raise children, and we can't make the sort of sacrifices that woman has made.' The other was much the same, except, 'We're old and in ill health, and we can't ...' But other readers wrote to say she had inspired them.

So let me be clear – I'm not saying *everyone* should be able to save this well. I'm just saying some determined people can achieve extraordinary savings. Here are a few:

True tale: Where there's a will there's a way

Sharil N of Auckland saves nearly two-thirds of her after-tax income. She says:

'I am on $45,000 after tax, but work six days a week, sometimes 12-hour shifts to get it. I live in Auckland on a $600 fortnightly budget which has allowed me to save $29,000 for the last few years, but it was less in previous years due to being on a lower income.

'Flatting helps keep rent costs down; living close to work keeps transport costs down; shopping in bulk, buying value brands and cooking at home helps the grocery bill. Little inconveniences equal big savings over time.'

Jo T and her partner, an Invercargill couple in their early thirties, are saving for a house:

'My partner earns a good income of $70,000 a year, which we can afford to live on comfortably for the two of us.

'Our idea is to save my income of $63,000 (around $40,000 cash in hand after KiwiSaver, student loans and tax) for the next two years. We have already saved $64,000 from living just off his income for the last two years when I was in a lower paying job.'

The woman who bought the Auckland house in 2018 while earning $30,000 says:

'Own a 14-year-old car and never eat out. Cook meals in batches to store in freezer. Always check pricing of meats, vegetables and fruits. Don't like alcohol, coffee and snacks. Make use of off-season deals when travelling once in two years. Avoid Boxing Day or Black Friday sales like a plague (haha).

'Switch power and internet to cheaper providers such as Flick and Big Pipe. Wear undergarments, clothes or shoes until seeing holes before replacing them. Always do window shopping for exercise purposes. Look for ways and means to save money, for example, cutting my own hair.

'Three years ago, bought a 4G Samsung mobile phone for $99 (on special offer) and top up $20 each year – meant for emergency use only.

'Have a weekly budget for groceries and challenge myself to spend less than that. Make sure each purchase is value for money i.e. watch every expense like a hawk!'

> **Moral:** If you really want to save, you'll find a way.

The over-savers

There are those who save too much. I've come across several over the years, and some people might call our champions above over-savers.

They are often single women, but not always. They want to be secure in their old age – which is fine of course – but are leading rather deprived lives in the meantime. For instance, some on pretty high incomes rarely spend much on going out. That's a real pity. They might get hit by the proverbial bus. Even if they don't, and live to a ripe old age, they've had too little fun in the meantime.

Important message to most readers: Please don't read this as 'permission' to spend more and save less – unless you are an over-saver.

How can you tell? If you expect to have a markedly higher standard of living in retirement than you have now, you're probably in that small group who I urge to get out there and live a bit more! You're probably healthier now than you'll be later, and you want to grab chances, as and when they arise, to enjoy life with family and friends.

True tale: 'I would love to travel, but ...'

A while back, a 40-year-old woman wrote to my *Weekend Herald* column. She's single, earns 'in the low six figures', owns her home and expects to be mortgage-free in 14 years. She has $50,000 in KiwiSaver, after withdrawing money to buy her home, and is contributing 8% of her pay towards it.

'I'm starting to wonder if I'm putting too much aside for retirement,' she wrote.

'I would love to travel and do some cosmetic upgrades to the house, but I'm quite conscious that the pension may not be available by the time I retire, and that I may have to rely on my own savings once I stop working.

'Should I reduce my KiwiSaver to 4% and use the extra income for things like travel and home maintenance, or invest that extra money another way, or just continue as I am?'

I did my best to reassure her that NZ Super will continue, even if at a slightly lower rate. (More on that in Step 7: 'Head confidently towards retirement – and through it'.) In light of that, I suggested she cut her KiwiSaver contributions to 3% and spend the extra take-home money on travel and other fun things.

When we were in touch again, some months later, she reported, 'I reduced my KiwiSaver, and am saving for a trip to Europe later this year, which I'm very excited about! I couldn't help but direct some of the savings into my mortgage, but I feel more relaxed about my retirement, whenever that may come about.'

Moral: Life is for living as well as for saving.

Where to save outside KiwiSaver: short-term savings

You've been setting aside money regularly. Great!

Every now and then – maybe every two months, or maybe when your savings account balance reaches $500 – transfer the money into an investment. But what investment?

That depends to a large extent on when you expect to spend the money.

If you think you are likely to spend it within two or three years, it's simplest to just use bank term deposits.

Is today's interest so terrible?

Figure 8: Inflation and interest rates – how times have changed

Inflation used to be higher than interest rates, but they swapped

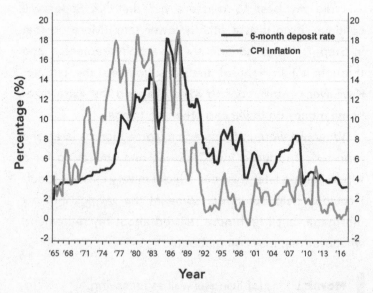

Source: Reserve Bank of NZ

Note: CPI inflation shows changes in the Consumer Price Index, which measures the changing prices of goods and services that New Zealanders buy.

I was once sailing in a small yacht through the narrow stretch of a harbour. The sails were full and we seemed to be going full-steam – sorry, full-sail – ahead. It felt great. But when we looked at the shoreline we realised we were actually going backwards. The force of the tide was stronger than the force of the wind.

Some time later, the wind had dropped and the tide had changed. The sailing wasn't nearly as exhilarating, but we were getting where we wanted to go.

Investing in bank term deposits in the late 1960s to early 1980s was like the first experience. It felt wonderful to earn interest well into the teens. Your savings balance zoomed up.

The only trouble was – as our graph shows – inflation was extremely high. This was partly because we 'imported' high US inflation, partly because of a huge oil price increase in 1973–74, and partly because of NZ government policies.

Importantly, inflation was higher than interest rates. Your $1,000 term deposit might be $1,120 a year later, but you could buy less with the $1,120 than you could with the $1,000 the year before. You were sailing backwards.

These days, your $1,000 might be just $1,030 a year later – at an interest rate of 3%. But with inflation below 2%, your buying power is growing. Your yacht is making progress.

And that's all that matters with money. As anyone who has used a foreign currency when travelling knows, it's not about the numbers, but what you can buy with your cash.

Let's add tax into the mix. In the bad old days, after paying lots of tax on your interest you were even further behind. These days, you pay much less tax on lower interest, so you can still come out ahead after tax.

Which bank term deposit?

- Don't just go with your own bank. Another bank is highly likely to offer a better interest rate. See what's being offered under the 'Saving' tab at www.interest.co.nz.

- Go to your own bank and ask if they can raise their rate to match the other bank. Several people have told me that worked for them.

- If you want a bit more sophistication, consider some alternatives with somewhat higher average returns. Some banks run what are called PIE term funds, which give many people a tax break. Or you could go into a cash fund, perhaps run by a KiwiSaver provider but not part of the KiwiSaver scheme, where your money isn't tied up. But in a cash fund your return will vary – which might be good or bad – and you'll pay fees.

Where to save outside KiwiSaver: mid-term savings

Bonds – remember them? They're like term deposits but issued by governments and companies. They work well for money you plan to spend in three to ten years.

You can buy bonds from a stockbroker, including online stockbroking services. Or, if that sounds too complicated, go for a bond fund. The fund manager will run it all for you, and you get a good spread of different bonds.

The next question is which bonds or which bond fund. We'll look at the funds first.

Remember back in Step 4 where we were finding the best type of KiwiSaver fund for you? Go through the same process, even though you're not going to use a KiwiSaver fund. This is because at this stage there's no non-KiwiSaver tool that works as well.

Answer the questions on when you're likely to spend the money and how much you can tolerate ups and downs in your balance. Let's say that leads you to decide to save in a balanced KiwiSaver fund. (This may well be a lower-risk fund than your earlier KiwiSaver choice, because you're planning to spend the money sooner.)

Next go through the same process as before to find which provider is right for you. With a different risk level, you might find a different provider is better.

Okay – you've now got a KiwiSaver fund selected, even though you don't want to put this money in KiwiSaver!

Look at that provider's website to see if they have a similar non-KiwiSaver fund. Most providers do. If you can't find that out easily, call or email them to ask.

Before committing to a fund, you'll want to check if they will accept contributions of the size and frequency you want to make. And how easy it is to get some or all of the money out whenever you want it. You might find it will take a few days for a withdrawal, but that probably won't be a problem.

Take note of how easy it is to deal with the provider. If they are slack, or use a lot of financial jargon you don't understand, give them a miss. Fund managers make plenty of money from you and me, and should make it easy for us to do business with them.

If you would prefer to invest in individual bonds, you can get a list of what's on the market at www.interest.co.nz.

Warning: This is a bit like a Maths alert but it's a Boredom alert. A friend reading this book told me this section made her want to put the book down. Horrors! If you're not interested in buying individual bonds, it's okay to skip down to the Rule of 72. But if you are a bond buyer, you'd better keep reading.

A key consideration when buying bonds is their credit rating, which is included on interest.co.nz.

Credit ratings are issued by three big international agencies: S&P, Moody's and Fitch. They give you a pretty good idea of how likely it is that you will get your interest and your money back.

S&P and Fitch's ratings range from AAA (extremely strong), through AA, A, BBB, BB, B and so on, down to D (in default). Moody's is similar, but they use Aaa, Aa, A, Baa, Ba, B and so on, down to C (in default).

Sometimes a rating has a plus or minus sign after it. Look at the letters first. For example, AA– is better than A+.

The Reserve Bank, which regulates our banks, points out that credit ratings are not like marks for an essay in high school, where a B was pretty good. Instead, a B credit rating means there's a one in five chance the institution will default over five years. I wouldn't take that on.

It's best to stick with what are called 'investment grade' bonds, which means they have a rating of BBB– (Baa if it's Moody's) or better. Bonds with lower ratings are sometimes called junk bonds. Note the name! They're not called that for nothing.

Banks get credit ratings. At the time of writing, the big four New Zealand banks – ANZ, ASB, BNZ and Westpac – all had an AA– rating. Kiwibank had A and TSB had A–. Cooperative, Heartland and SBS all had BBB.

For other companies, ratings include, for example, A– for Auckland International Airport, BBB+ for Genesis Energy and BBB for Chorus. Some smaller institutions have no rating. Unless you know a lot about them, give them a miss.

The agencies give these ratings based on research, but they're not perfect. In the global financial crisis of 2007–08, some highly rated companies went under. Still, the ratings generally give us good guidance.

For more on ratings and how to interpret them, see a clear explanation by the Reserve Bank at www.tinyurl.com/CreditNZ.

The Rule of 72

Maths alert!

The very handy Rule of 72 lets you quickly work out two things.

The first is roughly how long it will take for an investment to double. For example:

- If your investment is growing at 4% a year, divide 72 by 4. It will take 18 years to double.
- If you want to double your money in 10 years, divide 72 by 10. You will need to earn about 7% a year.

The second is useful if an investment that has doubled. Using the rule, you can work out roughly what return you've made. For example:

- If your house value has doubled over 12 years, divide 72 by 12, to get 6. The value has grown by 6% a year.
- If your share investment has doubled in 8 years, divide 72 by 8. The value has grown by 9% a year.

Note that the Rule of 72 works only for one-off investments – like buying a house or putting a lump sum into an investment. It doesn't work for KiwiSaver or any other investment where you drip-feed in money over time.

The rule is an approximation. It's most accurate for returns of 6% to 10%, and gets a bit dodgy for returns of less than 3% or more than 15%. If your house value has doubled in two years – which has occasionally happened recently – the rule says your annual return is 36%, but it's actually more like 41%. Still, it gives you a pretty good idea.

One of the beauties of the rule is that you can divide 72 by 2, 3, 4, 6, 8, 9, 12, 18, 24 and 36, which makes calculations easier. And for other numbers, near enough is good enough.

Main point (for those who don't like maths): This gives you a rough idea of how the numbers are working for you. But if it's all too hard, forget it!

Where to save outside KiwiSaver: longer-term savings

We saw in the KiwiSaver step that it's good to go for riskier investments over the long term. Your returns will probably be higher, and there's time to recover from a downturn.

If you have money you want to tie up for a decade or more outside KiwiSaver, the same thing applies. And for most people a riskier managed fund is the best bet.

Go through the same process as outlined above for mid-term savings. Use the KiwiSaver online tools to find the best KiwiSaver fund for your long-term money, and then see if that provider offers a similar non-KiwiSaver fund.

As with mid-term savings, check if the fund you're considering will accept contributions of the size and frequency that suit you. And check how easy it is to withdraw money.

Not just New Zealand

Remember back when we were talking about choosing a KiwiSaver fund and I said it's good if your fund has a fair bit of its share and bond investments offshore? Let's look at this in a bit more depth.

There are two main reasons for investing beyond New Zealand. And they're both about reducing risk. So if you're thinking overseas investments add to your risk, think again.

Reason 1: Diversification

This means spreading your risk over lots of different investments. This idea will crop up several more times in this book. It's really important. But here we're talking about a specific type of diversification – spreading your investments around the world.

If you took the value of all the shares traded on the New Zealand stock exchange, the NZX, the total would be about 0.1% of all the shares in the world. That's not one in a hundred, that's one in a thousand. Our share market is, to put it rudely, a minnow.

What's more, there are many industries not represented amongst NZ shares, such as cars and major electronic goods. If you confine yourself to local shares, you'll miss out on what could be the biggest growth shares.

Some people say it's good to stick with New Zealand shares because of what's called *dividend imputation*. This is a tax credit that recognises that companies pay tax on their profits, so it's unfair if dividends paid out of those profits are then taxed again in the hands of shareholders. But imputation is not a powerful enough reason not to invest overseas. It's more than offset by the advantages of diversification.

When you stop to think about it, you probably have a job, perhaps a house, perhaps even more than one property in this country. That's enough exposure to a single economy that could be crippled by an agricultural disease or a major earthquake or volcanic eruption.

It's far safer to have some of your assets in other economies. And not just Australia. Some New Zealanders say they feel safer investing in Australia than further afield. But the Aussie and New Zealand share markets tend to move somewhat similarly. And, again, you still won't cover a wide range of industries if you confine your offshore investing to Australia.

Put some of your savings in international investments and there's a good chance that when our share market falls, that will be offset by gains elsewhere. Sure, the reverse happens too – that New Zealand gains can be pulled down by losses overseas. But over the long run your ride should be somewhat smoother if your investments range far and wide.

Points to notice about Figure 9:

- NZ and overseas shares sometimes follow similar paths, but sometimes very different paths.
- In both cases, there are lots of ups and downs – including some serious falls over a couple of years following really strong rises. But in the long run the trend is upwards. Figure 9 shows that if you invested $1,000 in NZ shares in 1970, and left it there to grow, reinvesting your dividends, it would have grown to $91,000 after tax. In overseas shares it would have grown to $43,000. Still pretty impressive.
- While NZ shares have grown much faster than world shares in the past decade, that could easily change.

Figure 9: Share markets don't move together

Value of $1,000 invested in 1973 in NZ and overseas shares, including dividends (after tax)

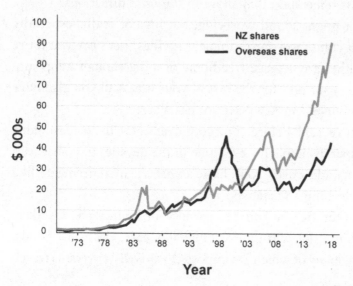

Source: MCA

Technical stuff: The calculations for this graph don't include costs of investing, such as brokerage if you invest directly in shares or fees if you invest in a share fund. That would reduce returns quite a lot over a long period. But they do include tax at the top PIR rate of 28% (income over $48,000). Returns would be higher for those on lower incomes, because their tax rate would be lower. NZ shares include calculations for imputation credits, as they are part of income.

If we look back there are periods, like the late 1990s, when overseas shares grew way faster – more than doubling in just a few years. That could happen again at some point. We just don't know.

Reason 2: Dollar movements

The second reason to invest offshore is to do with foreign exchange rates – the fact that the Kiwi dollar fluctuates against other dollars.

If the value of our dollar falls against other currencies, the value of any investments you have offshore rises. And the reverse also happens – if our dollar rises, offshore investments fall. Just remember: they move in *opposite* directions.

That might sound worrying, but it's not really, especially when it comes to your retirement savings. Let's say you retire with either a mortgage-free home or a big enough lump sum to cover your rent for the rest of your life. And you also have other savings – in KiwiSaver or elsewhere.

As I've said before, I'm confident there'll be reasonable NZ Super available for everyone in the decades to come. And Super should cover your basic expenses in retirement, like food, clothing and transport.

So what are you going to spend your savings on? It's likely that quite a lot will go on things like cars, electronic goods, books – many of which are imported – as well as overseas travel.

What if the Kiwi dollar falls between now and when you spend this money? The prices of imported goods and foreign travel will rise. But, as we said above, the value of your overseas investments will also rise. That will help you pay the extra for the imports and travel. It's a bonus you wouldn't have had if you had stuck with just New Zealand investments.

What about the reverse? If the Kiwi dollar rises, the value of your overseas investments will fall. But the price of imports and travel will also fall (because of the rise in the Kiwi), so you won't suffer.

Confused? Some people can get their heads around this and some can't. But don't worry. All you really need to know is that if you want to spend a fair bit of your savings on imports and foreign travel, you actually lower your risk by having some of your savings overseas.

But isn't offshore investing disloyal?

Some people say we should stick with investing in New Zealand to support our companies. But I disagree. We talked earlier about disasters that could hit our economy. If an agricultural disease or natural disaster struck, it would be great if many people had offshore investments that held their value. They could then bring some money home to help get things going again here.

Even if something like that never happens – here's hoping! – if many people are better off because they have invested overseas, that helps the whole country.

How to invest offshore

You could go to a sharebroker and ask them to sell you shares in, say, some US companies. That's what some seriously wealthy people do. But I don't recommend it if you want to keep your investing simple. Investing directly overseas makes things more complicated. Taxes are tricky and you will almost certainly need to hire an expert to handle them. And after you die it takes longer for your estate to be settled if you have overseas investments.

It's easier if you invest in a New Zealand-based fund manager which, in turn, invests in overseas assets. Let them handle the tax complications and so on. Many local fund managers offer international share or bond funds, giving you ownership of teeny proportions of some of the world's biggest companies.

How much of your savings should be offshore? That really depends on the proportion you expect to spend on imports and travel. For many New Zealanders it should be at least half your long-term savings – in or out of KiwiSaver.

Other investments – individual shares and rental property

How come I haven't suggested individual shares or rental property for longer-term savings? Both can be good investments, but ...

Individual shares

I'm not keen on sending you off to a sharebroker – online or otherwise – to buy shares in This Company or That Company. Unless you have, say, $100,000 or more, you can't realistically buy shares in a wide range of companies. And concentrating on a few shares raises your risk. It's great if they do well, but they could easily not.

Remember I said back in the KiwiSaver step that most people – arguably everyone – is no good at consistently picking which shares will do well. If the experts can't do it, do you really think you can?

I often hear from people who say something like, 'Hang on a minute. I've invested directly in shares and look how well I've done over the last ten years.' What they don't realise is that the share markets as a whole have been performing well. Everyone in share funds has also seen their investments rise healthily. In fact, any direct share investor who hasn't done well over that period should be ashamed!

There's another issue, too. If you own your own shares, you need to keep track of dividends, and sometimes there are issues on which shareholders are asked to vote and other complications. Some people – like my father – make a hobby of following all that. But most of us are better off in a share fund, leaving the managers to deal with that stuff.

Grab the bargains

Every now and then you'll either be given shares or get an opportunity to buy them at below market price. It might be because a power company or insurance company is changing its structure, or your employer is offering you shares in the company.

Generally, I would grab those chances. But then sell the shares as soon as you can.

If it's an employee stock ownership plan, the company may require you to keep the shares for several years. Your bosses want you to feel more involved in the company as one of its owners. And I have to say that when I've been in one of these schemes it did work to some extent; I wanted the company to do well.

But still, I suggest you sell when you're allowed to. Let's say the shares are worth $1,000. Consider what you would do if you inherited $1,000 in cash. Would you invest it in your employer's shares if you were buying them at the market price? Almost certainly not. So don't hold on to them. Sell them and perhaps invest in a share fund.

Rental property

Ah, rental property! It's the great love of many New Zealanders, quite likely including you or your parents or friends. And there's no denying that a lot of people have profited handsomely from investing in rentals.

Perhaps because of that, over my years as a columnist, the harshest criticism levelled at me has come from big fans of rental property. I've 'got it in for' property, they say. None of them has ever come up with why I would be that way. I don't get anything – money or love – out of being 'anti-property'.

The fact is that I'm not anti it. I did do disastrously with one house – which you'll read about shortly. But apart from that, I've done really well out of buying and selling homes over the years. The value of one property, in Sydney, almost doubled in just two years.

We should all be wary, though, of stories about huge gains people have made in property. The gains on your home can be pretty meaningless if you're selling it and buying another in the same market. Both prices have risen, and you're not really getting ahead.

But with rentals, the stories sound wonderful. We've all heard people say they bought a property for, say, $300,000, and sold it just three years later for twice that – sometimes even more.

I've got three responses to that:

- They had good luck with their timing. The property market happened to rise fast in that period – perhaps boosted by a rare plunge in mortgage interest rates like the one we saw in 2008–09. We won't see that again for a long time, because rates can't go down much more than they are now.
- They are perhaps not telling you about their other property investment in a different period, when the value fell or went sideways.
- People often forget about all the money they've put into a rental property while they owned it. It's common for mortgage payments to be bigger than rental income. And then there's rates and insurance, plus occasional large sums for repairs or to redecorate. If you buy a property for $500,000 and then spend $300,000 on it and sell it for $900,000, you didn't make $400,000. Oh, and by the way, your profit should be taxable, and it's increasingly likely that will be policed.

The thing about property is that while some people do really well out of it, it's riskier and more complicated than many people realise. Everyone knows shares are risky, but rental property can be more so. Read on.

When borrowing to invest goes wrong

Most people have to borrow to buy rental property. Sure, you borrow to buy your own home too. It's a rare bird who buys their home with cash. But the very fact that you've borrowed to buy your home means it's not a great idea to boost the borrowing to buy a rental property as well.

Gearing is great when things go well. You get the gain not only on the money you put in, but also on the bank's money. Some people have built fortunes on this. But gearing is a bit like Henry Wadsworth Longfellow's little girl – 'When she was good she was very good indeed, but when she was bad she was horrid.'

This applies to borrowing to invest in anything – shares, emus or property. But few people borrow to invest in shares or emus. Gearing is mainly a property thing. And, as Figure 10 shows, the more you gear, the more you stand to gain – or lose.

Before you start to look at Figure 10, note that it simplifies things. To make it easier to follow, we don't bother with interest on the loans, or loan repayments, until you sell. (After Figure 10, we'll look at how including those would affect things. But for now, please bear with me!)

In Figure 10, you start with savings of $100,000.

With *no gearing*, in our lucky scenario the balance rises by 20% to $120,000. There's no loan to pay back, so you end up with the $120,000. But in our unlucky scenario, the balance falls by 20% over time. You end up with just $80,000.

Next we look at *light gearing*. In the lucky scenario, the investment gains 20% so you end up with $240,000. After you pay back the $100,000 loan, you have $140,000 left. Your original $100,000 has grown by 40%. You've done twice as well as you would have with no gearing. Great!

But if things go badly – as in the unlucky scenario – your $200,000 drops 20% to just $160,000. And that's not all. By the time you pay back the $100,000 loan, you're left with just

Figure 10: What happens when you gear

The lucky geared investor: starting with $100,000

	No gearing	Light gearing	Heavy gearing
Amount invested	$100,000	$100,000 + $100,000 loan = $200,000	$100,000 + $900,000 loan = $1 million
Value after <u>20% gain</u>	$120,000	$240,000	$1.2 million
Value after you sell and pay off loan	$120,000	$240,000 – $100,000 loan = $140,000	$1.2 million – $900,000 loan = $300,000
Your $100,000 has ...	... grown 20%	... grown 40%	... tripled!

The unlucky geared investor: starting with $100,000

	No gearing	Light gearing	Heavy gearing
Amount invested	$100,000	$100,000 + $100,000 loan = $200,000	$100,000 + $900,000 loan = $1 million
Value after <u>20% loss</u>	$80,000	$160,000	$800,000
Value after you sell and pay off loan	$80,000	$160,000 – $100,000 loan = $60,000	$800,000 – $900,000 loan = debt of $100,000
Your $100,000 has ...	... lost 20%	... lost 40%	... disappeared, and you still owe $100,000!

$60,000. That's 40% down on your original $100,000. Not so great.

Heavy gearing is typically for buying property. In the lucky scenario, after a 20% gain, your $1 million has turned into $1.2 million. You pay back the $900,000 loan and are left with $300,000. Your original $100,000 has tripled. Wow! That's way better than with no or low gearing.

But the unlucky scenario is very unlucky. A 20% loss turns your $1 million into just $800,000. And then you've got to repay a $900,000 loan. You sell the property for $800,000, but you've still got to come up with another $100,000 from somewhere else. Things have gone horribly wrong. *The heavier the gearing, the bigger the risk.*

Maths alert! As noted above, the tables in Figure 10 don't include interest, or loan repayments until you sell. If we included interest, the gains from gearing would be smaller and the losses bigger. But this would often be offset by rental income (or if you had borrowed to invest in shares, dividends.) So it probably wouldn't make much difference to the outcomes in the tables. It would just make it much harder to follow!

If we included loan repayments, that's really just a separate savings program. For every dollar you repay, you have one more dollar of equity in the property, and so you reduce your gearing. But it doesn't affect the basic idea of gearing.

Main point: Gearing makes a good investment better, but a bad investment worse. In other words, it increases your risk.

'Sure,' say the keen rental folk, 'but you don't make losses on rental property.'

Let me paint a few pictures. What if ...

You have to put extra into your mortgage payments because the rental income isn't enough – a common situation –

and you lose your job? Or the tenants stop paying? (Even the nicest ones might suffer a cash crisis.) Or you don't have any tenants for a while because you can't find good ones? Or you find the house is leaky – or worse still, all three units you bought in a new high-rise are leaky? Or the place has been used as a meth lab, or for any number of other reasons you suddenly need to spend a lot on it? Or mortgage interest rates rise fast. Just ten years ago, average two-year fixed mortgage interest rates were above 9% and floating rates were above 10%. It could happen again.

And what if several of those disasters happen at once?

All sorts of situations arise in which landlords find they have to sell their rental property unexpectedly, quite often when the economy isn't great. That may be why you lost your job and your tenant lost their job in the first place. And, contrary to popular belief, property prices sometimes fall. It's odd how quickly people forget that, but it does happen, as Figure 11 shows.

Every time there's a property downturn, not only are some landlords forced to sell, but they sell for less than their mortgage. They end up with no asset and a debt. I've known people that has happened to. It's not pretty.

Figure 11 shows ordinary house prices and also house prices that have been adjusted for inflation. That second lower line shows how much house prices have grown when we remove inflation from the mix.

Back in the 1970s and 1980s, inflation was high – as you can see by the big gap between the two lines. So, ordinary house prices didn't fall, although prices adjusted for inflation did quite often. Now, with inflation much lower, even ordinary house prices have fallen (the line drops below zero) several times in the past 30 years.

Figure 11: House prices sometimes fall

When line goes below zero, prices have fallen

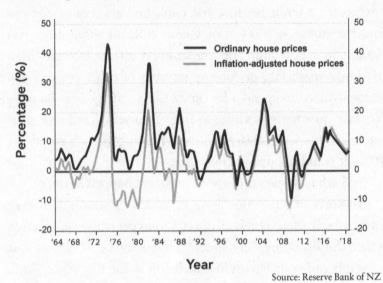

Source: Reserve Bank of NZ

Other downsides of rental property

- Being a landlord can be a hassle. If something goes wrong with the property or with the tenants, you'd better get it fixed fast. Of course you can hire a company to do that, but their fee eats a big hole in your profits.

- Government changes. Politicians of all stripes have been saying for years that too many New Zealanders put their savings into rental properties. So the politicians are constantly looking into changing mortgage rules, housing standards and taxes to discourage that. Changes made in March 2018 have meant that gains on newly bought rentals that are resold within five years are taxed. Also, under mortgage regulations, you usually need a much bigger deposit to buy a rental than to buy your own home. The trend towards more regulation is likely to continue.

- It's more complicated to get cash out of a property investment than out of shares or a share fund. Also, it usually takes a lot longer to sell a rental property. If you need the money in a hurry, you could find yourself selling the rental for a low price.

- Lack of diversification. If you own your own home and a rental, you've got a huge exposure to property. And if the rental is near your home – and understandably many people like that – you'll be hit doubly if values in the area deteriorate. That does happen – in any neighbourhood. (See 'True Tale', page 140.) To avoid that risk, you could buy your rental somewhere distant from your home. But then you're not Johnny on the Spot when things go wrong.

- You can't drip-feed into the investment. Many people think they can pick the best time to buy a property, but they're often wrong. Timing any market is pretty much impossible. (More on this in Step 6: 'Stay cool'.) A good way to get around this problem is to drip-feed your money into an investment, but you can't do that with property. And if prices fall soon after you purchase, it's much harder to sell later at a gain.

If you want to go ahead anyway

Having said all that, rental property works well for some people – particularly those who enjoy maintenance work and doing up houses, and are happy about being firm with difficult tenants.

If you're already a landlord, good on you! I hope none of the bad things listed above ever happen to you. If you're just at the 'thinking about it' stage, be aware of what you might be getting yourself into.

Some rules for the determined would-be landlord:

- Avoid buying when everyone else is buying – or has bought recently. If you're jumping on a bandwagon, you're likely to pay too much.
- Avoid mortgaging your home to buy a rental. If things go wrong, you could end up losing your home.
- Plan your cash flow – when the dollars will come in and when they will go out. Flick back a few pages to the heading 'When borrowing to invest goes wrong', and find the paragraph that starts 'Let me paint a few pictures' (page 136). How would you cope, cashwise, if one or more of those bad things happens? It's wise to work through a worst case scenario.

True tale: Can you top this loss?

The biggest loss I've ever taken on a property was in the smart Auckland suburb of St Heliers. We had bought the house for $385,000 just before the 1987 share market crash.

A couple of years later we wanted to move elsewhere. To our dismay, we got only $270,000 for the place – a 30% drop. How come? A lot of people in that suburb had been ruined by the crash and had to sell their houses in a hurry, and that had dragged down the market.

Moral: House values can fall a long way even in 'nice' suburbs.

What about gold and other investments?

Every now and then, usually when the share market has the wobbles, some people rush to invest in gold. They say things like, 'It's the only investment you can count on if the world falls apart.'

Really? After Armageddon, when nobody has shelter or enough to eat, what good will a chunk of shiny metal be? As Warren Buffett has put it, 'Gold gets dug out of the ground in Africa, or someplace. Then we melt it down, dig another hole, bury it again and pay people to stand around guarding it. It has no utility. anyone watching from Mars would be scratching their head.'

Some people debate this, but in any case we're assuming your gold investment is actually in the metal itself, as opposed to the more common form of gold investment – in a gold fund or similar. That would be as useless as shares.

The facts are:

- The gold price is as volatile as share prices. Big drops are not uncommon. And the price tends to keep falling for much longer than share prices.
- Gold doesn't produce any ongoing returns. Bonds pay interest, shares give you dividends, property gives you rent, but gold gives you nothing until you sell it – hopefully at a gain. If prices have fallen when you have to sell, it could look like a pretty lousy investment.

Having said that, if you really want to put a small percentage of your savings in gold, I wouldn't argue with you. To some extent gold rises when shares fall, and the reverse, so it does spread your risk a bit.

Many other investments, though, are just fads. People have made and then lost a lot on things like emus. What about bitcoin and other cryptocurrencies? The jury is still out. If I say, 'Give it a miss', and then you hear of people making huge profits, you might get mad at me. But then again you might be really glad you read this warning. Let's just say I'm staying away.

If you have a problem

Stuck in a battle with a bank, insurance company, financial adviser, stockbroker, credit union, KiwiSaver provider, lender, credit card provider, finance company or anyone else who provides a financial service in New Zealand? One of the country's four financial dispute resolution schemes may be able to help you. And their help is free.

The four schemes are:

- Banking Ombudsman Scheme (BOS);
- Financial Dispute Resolution Service (FDRS);
- Financial Services Complaints Ltd (FSCL); and
- Insurance and Financial Services Ombudsman (IFSO).

Every financial services provider has to belong to one of the schemes, and has to tell you which one it belongs to. In many cases it will be written on their website or in their literature. You can also find out by looking at the register on the Companies Office website, at www.tinyurl.com/NZRegister.

Before you approach the scheme, you have to discuss your problem with the financial company. But if you're not happy with how it's been resolved, it's time to go to the dispute resolution scheme. You'll be asked for your side of the story, and so will the provider. The scheme then makes a decision that the provider can't wriggle out of. But if you're unhappy with it, you are free to take other action, such as going to court.

The schemes pride themselves on being fair to both sides of a dispute. However, at first glance the figures on their decisions might seem discouraging to consumers, as more decisions tend to go against consumers than for them (although many decisions are half and half). But this is because, if the provider has clearly been wrong, they will tend to settle a dispute before it gets to their dispute resolution scheme.

Still, there are many decisions fully or partly in favour of the consumer. And even when that's not the case, many consumers have reported they are content with the outcome because they've learnt more about why the problem arose.

For more on how the schemes work, and examples of cases they've looked into, see their websites. There are some fascinating stories there.

Disclosure: I'm on the board of FSCL, representing consumers, and I used to be on the board of the Banking Ombudsman Scheme. If they were for-profit organisations, I could be accused here of trying to drum up business for them. But they're not!

I think what the four schemes do is great, but their work is too little known. I urge you to use them when you need to, and to tell others about them.

Steering clear of scams

While dispute resolution schemes can help you with problems with New Zealand-based financial services providers, usually they can't help if you've been ripped off by a locally based crook. And they almost certainly can't help if it's an offshore company. You'll have to go to the police or a government agency – and even then you might find they can't do much, especially if it's an overseas scam.

It's far better to avoid being ripped off than to try to remedy things after the fact.

9 warning signs of scams

Here are some flashing lights that say, 'Keep away!'

Warning sign 1: The return is expected to be higher than, say, 10% a year

If they say the investment is also low-risk, be extra wary.

There are some ridiculous examples out there. One Australian share trading program offered 890% a year. That means that if you invested $1 and waited 15 years, you would have six times the value of all the world's goods and services produced in a year.

But more sophisticated scammers make it look less ridiculous. Bernie Madoff – the American who confessed in 2009 to running the largest financial fraud in US history – said he was giving investors a return of about 1% a month, with no losses for 20 years. You can't get that high a return without ups and downs, but investors were ever hopeful.

Warning sign 2: Very high past returns

Scammers will tell you they've made huge returns. Sometimes they are just lying. Other times they have very carefully picked a particular period to present to you. You can be sure that over the long term, the story would be quite different.

Warning sign 3: Pressure to commit quickly

The salesperson will tell you there are only a few places left, or it's cheaper if you enrol now. They know that if you go away and think about it, you might get talked out of it, or simply come to your senses. They will do anything to get you to make a quick decision.

Set yourself a rule to *always* say 'No' when pressured – or at least say you need a few days before you decide. This is easier said than done. You get a horrible feeling that you're going to miss out and will deeply regret it. Believe me – you are much more likely to regret it if you commit on the spot.

There are many good investments out there that don't require a quick decision. And arguably none that do.

Warning sign 4: A stranger approaches you – by phone, email, social media, snail mail, in a mall, wherever – with an irresistible offer, perhaps at 'below value'

Through my columns, and at many seminars, I've asked if anyone has ever done well from an investment that began with the company approaching them. Nobody has ever said yes – although quite a few have said the opposite.

Always think about why someone is giving you this great opportunity to get rich. If it's so good, why don't they just keep it to themselves, and borrow as much as they can to invest? Could it be because, by selling you the investment, they are the ones getting rich?

Warning sign 5: Free or nearly free seminars.

Again, why are they doing this for you? A common tactic is to entice you along and then talk you into signing up for further expensive courses or financial advice or an investment. Once they've got you in the room, they can be pretty persuasive.

(By the way, just because someone charges for a seminar, that doesn't necessarily mean it isn't also a con. It must be wonderful for them, getting revenue for the seminar as well as making heaps later!)

Warning sign 6: A 'black box' you don't fully understand – such as a computer program or app – that gives you high returns with low risk

I've been to a few seminars offering these. 'All you have to do is pay up for the magic, and then trade shares (or options or bitcoin or whatever) according to what the black box tells you to do, and you'll make much more money than you lose.' They 'prove' it works by showing you some successful recent trades. They don't, of course, show you the other unsuccessful ones. But it's not that obvious. These folk are clever.

As we'll discuss later, frequent trading of any investment is almost always a loser's game. And no black box can change that.

Warning sign 7: Requests for PIN numbers, passwords or usernames

Sometimes these come in phone calls or emails supposedly from your bank or credit card provider or other legitimate business. But banks and the like never ask for that info. Keep it to yourself.

Warning sign 8: 'You've won a prize', but you didn't enter

These come by snail mail or online. You've never heard of this outfit, but it's still got a wonderful prize to give you. Funny, though, they always seem to end up asking you for money before they give you any – which you don't ever receive.

Warning sign 9: A request to keep an investment opportunity private or secret

The people who make such requests do it in a way that makes you feel special and privileged. After all, not everyone gets the chance to share in a Nigerian official's millions. Secrecy is a great way to keep you from checking with an accountant or lawyer.

The man who could pick shares perfectly

A conman selects ten shares.

He emails a million people, saying Share 1 will do very well, another million people, saying Share 2 will do very well etc.

Second round: He then targets the million whose share performed best. He selects another ten shares, and sends 100,000 people a recommendation on Share 11, and another 100,000 on Share 12 etc.

Third round: He targets the 100,000 whose second share also did well. He selects another ten shares, and sends 10,000 people a tip on Share 21, and sends another 10,000 a tip on Share 22 etc.

Can you see where this is going? By the next round, he has 1,000 people who are deeply impressed. After all, for them he has picked four shares that were big winners. Of course they are going to invest a lot with him ...

False friends – taking comfort when you shouldn't

Scammers have clever ways of making you feel everything is okay. Here are some of them:

- They run ads in reputable publications, TV or radio. You might trust the paper or whatever, but their advertising salespeople don't have the time to check the credentials of advertisers.
- They use wording like: 'It's completely legal', 'Approved by [a government agency or Consumer NZ or similar].' These are usually empty words. Note that the government and Consumer NZ don't approve investments.
- They offer a money-back guarantee. But that's useful only if the company still exists when you want to claim. Even if they do still exist, they tell you that you haven't followed all the rules so the guarantee is not valid.
- They recommend that you check the investment with your lawyer or accountant – knowing that you'll probably think, 'If they say that, the investment must be solid, so I won't bother.' Do bother. And by the way, don't ever use the lawyer or accountant they provide. Even if they are qualified, they're hardly going to give you an unbiased view of an investment, with your interests at heart.
- They list impressive testimonials. But are the people real? And if they are, are they the promoters' relatives and friends?
- They offer referrals from 'independent' offices or websites that aren't independent. If they say a

reputable company recommends them, check with that company. I know of cases where the company says they've never heard of the promoter or the investment.

- They use classy-looking literature printed on high-quality paper. Anyone can do that, especially if they're making lots of money from fools.
- They guarantee that if you buy one of their units or apartments you will receive rent of at least $X for several years. The rent is high, and if it's guaranteed, the investment must be good, right? After the guarantee period ends, you discover the rent the tenant is actually paying is much lower. The promoter has been subsidising the rent, using a small portion of the profits it made because you paid over the top for the property.
- They create websites and even fake government authorities to give the impression that they are legitimate. I've seen some pretty convincing ones. Mind you, not all fake websites are created by the bad guys. Check out www.howeycoins.com, which looks like it's offering a wonderful ICO (initial coin offering) investment. But if you click on 'Buy Coins Now!' you land on the website of the US government's Securities and Exchange Commission, with the following message: 'If you responded to an investment offer like this, you could have been scammed – HoweyCoins are completely fake!' It's a great way of warning people.
- The nastiest of all – they befriend you, perhaps on a dating website. You correspond for some time, and may even have long phone conversations. You've

found the love of your life, and will meet them in person soon, but they're overseas. Suddenly they email to say they're in a spot of bother, and could you possibly lend them some money, just for a short time. That's the last you hear of them – except perhaps for a request for further money.

Another 'false friend' situation is when a real friend of yours, often a community or church leader, recommends an investment. It's been great for them, but it's a flop for you. Has your friend lied to you? Probably not.

This is what is sometimes called *affinity fraud*. The promoter approaches the community leader and offers them a really good deal. The promoter then puts in plenty of their own money to make sure the leader gets great returns. It's an 'investment' by the promoter, who can then rip off all the people the leader brings into the scheme.

This is a particularly horrible scenario. It must make the leader feel terrible. And it invites the rest of us to not trust our friends. Let's not let this stuff happen. Friends are great for many things, but not usually for hot investments.

How Bernie Madoff made off with smart people's money

US psychology professor and author Robert Cialdini made some fascinating comments in America's *Wall Street Journal* about Bernie Madoff and his hedge fund. In the following quote, I've put some phrases in italics, for emphasis.

The 'murkiness' of a hedge fund, said Cialdini, makes investors feel that it is 'the inherent domain of *people who know more than we do* ... This uncertainty leads us to look for social proof: *evidence that other people we trust* have already decided to invest. And by playing up how exclusive his funds were, Mr Madoff shifted investors' fears from the risk that they might lose money to the *risk they might lose out on making money.*

'If you did get invited in, then you were *anointed a member* of this particular club of "sophisticated investors".' Once someone you respect went out of his way to grant you access, says Professor Cialdini, it would *seem almost an 'insult' to do any further investigation.* 'Mr. Madoff also was known to *throw investors out of his funds* for asking too many questions, so no one wanted to rock the boat.'

Other tips

1 The early bird gets the bucks

Affinity fraud isn't the only situation where the first people in the investment do really well. In *Ponzi schemes*, the early investors think they're getting high returns and tell others about the scheme. In fact, their 'returns' are partly or fully made up of the money later investors put in – after the promoters have creamed off their take. In the end, the music stops, and more recent investors get off the roundabout with little or nothing.

While Ponzi schemes are illegal, *pyramid schemes* aren't necessarily. In pyramid schemes, early investors or purchasers are rewarded for recruiting others – we'll call the new recruits the second tier. Then the second tier recruit more people to make up the third tier, and the first and second tiers are rewarded for that. Then the third tier recruits more people, and the first, second and third tiers are rewarded. And on and on it goes.

The top-tier people make a lot of money, and the second tier also does pretty well. But by the time you get down a few tiers, there's not much to go around.

I don't like the way these schemes work. I suggest you give a miss to any scheme in which you are expected to recruit others.

2 Trouble in your inbox

Surely everyone knows about this stuff by now. But apparently not. If something enticing comes in by email, look closely at the sender's address. And if you're redirected to a website, look closely at the actual URL to confirm it's legitimate. Scammers often use names that look very like legitimate names. If you have any doubts, phone the organisation, using a phone number you got from somewhere other than the website. Better still, just give any email offer a miss.

3 Take care with your personal info

The 2018 scandal with Facebook has made everyone more wary about what personal information they put online. But still, we can let info slip without realising it – even in phone calls. Somebody might 'innocently' ask if you have a cat or a dog, and if so what's its name. Or they say, 'I think my mum went to school with your mum. What was her maiden name?' And they've got part of your password!

You can be caught out, too, if you've been asleep. I heard of a man who was woken by a 6 am phone call. 'I'm calling from Visa,' said the voice. 'Someone is using your credit card in Turkey. I just need you to verify your details.' The drowsy man said too much before he had a chance to think about what he was doing.

4 Suspicious?

Do an internet search on the business name coupled with the words 'scam' or 'review'. If you find damaging information on the company, obviously give it a miss. But if you find only good info, that doesn't necessarily mean all is well.

Two websites you can rely on are run by Consumer Affairs and the Financial Markets Authority. On www.consumeraffairs.govt.nz, click on Scamwatch. This tells you, 'How to recognise, avoid, and take action against scams, protect personal information, and prevent identity theft both online and offline.' It has lots of readable and useful info, including 'Report a scam'. Do!

On www.fma.govt.nz, do a search for 'scams'. That will give you types of scams, how to avoid them, and info on specific named investments to avoid (but don't be comforted if a company isn't listed there).

Above all else ...

Perhaps rule number one in the fight against scams is: Never invest in anything if you don't fully understand where the returns come from.

We know that interest we earn on a term deposit comes from the bank rewarding us for having the use of our money for a while. We know that with property we will earn rental income and hopefully a gain when we sell. We know that with shares or a share fund we will earn dividends and, again, hopefully a gain when we sell. But what about, say, binary options – which were being sold by swindlers recently? How do they generate wealth?

With many scams, it's not clear where the returns are coming from. That probably means they won't actually come.

True tale: Not even the salesman understood

Some years ago a friend of a friend asked me to go with her to a free seminar about an 'investment opportunity'. It was something to do with property, but it was complicated. I couldn't understand where the promised high returns were coming from.

After the main guy presented his persuasive spiel, the audience was broken up into small groups, each with a salesperson to answer our questions and sign us up. I asked lots of questions, and I soon became convinced that the salesperson didn't understand where the returns came from either. But he was clever at hiding it.

The others in my group soon became impatient with me. My irritating questions were probably planting doubts in their minds, putting stumbling blocks across their pathway to wealth. I soon gave up, but as I walked away – taking my friend with me – I saw several others in my group lining up to sign on the dotted line.

I don't know how they did. The whole outfit seemed to disappear from the limelight soon after that. But it's not hard to guess.

Looking back, I'm sure the whole scheme was *deliberately* confusing. Put lots of numbers on a whiteboard, move them around and spout lots of complicated financial words, and write '12%' at the bottom. The suckers will sign up.

But not you!

Moral: If it's unclear, give it a miss.

Step 5 check

Have you:

- ❏ Set a savings goal?
- ❏ Paid yourself first?
- ❏ Promised that you'll save more whenever your costs or taxes fall, or you get a lump sum or pay rise?
- ❏ Worked out the best investment for your savings?
- ❏ Ventured offshore?
- ❏ Thought hard before going into individual shares or a rental?
- ❏ Learnt how not to be scammed?

Reward

Chocolates, cheese or flowers; or a 'me day' with a walk, book, time with family, being creative; or donating to a charity, or anything else that makes you smile.

What's next? All this saving is great, but how do you deal with market ups and downs?

Step
6

STAY COOL

In which we ...

- Learn how and why you should spread your money around ...
- ... And don't look over your shoulder
- ... And forget about timing the markets
- ... And keep risk down so YOU choose when to sell
- ... And – best of all – relax
- Look into our minds, and understand why we make bad investment decisions
- Discover how men's and women's investments differ

This book is about investing easily. That means not worrying about your money. 'That's all very well,' you may be saying. 'I don't worry when everything's going smoothly. But when every newspaper and news bulletin is screaming "'Crash!", and telling me how much the average person in KiwiSaver has lost, of course I'm going to fret. Wouldn't you?' At the risk of sounding smug, my reply is, 'Nope!'

Even when the markets are misbehaving, if you follow the five rules in this step, you should also be able to stay cool.

Before we start, though, I should note that I've seen so-called experts challenging every one of these rules. Often they have a vested interest. They'll make more money out of you if you trade frequently, for example. But still they can sound pretty credible.

So why listen to me? I first learnt these rules quite a few decades ago when I was studying for my MBA. I was working full time as a financial reporter for the *Chicago Tribune*, and after work, at about 5.30 pm on one or two nights a week, you could have seen me trudging along Michigan Avenue, textbooks under one arm, to the University of Chicago's downtown Business School. Most of the university's MBA students studied full time on campus. But I was one of a growing number who attended evening lectures, one or two courses at a time.

It wasn't always easy to pay attention through lectures from 6 to 9 pm, with one coffee break, after a full day's work. But the lectures I had no trouble staying awake through were those from a professor called Merton Miller.

Mert had made a deal with the university. He would teach an evening course only if someone would bring a cold beer into the lecture theatre for him partway through. Beer can in hand, he taught us finance, and clearly loved his subject. He knew many people in financial circles, and told lots of 'war stories' about how some academic theories didn't work in practice, but the ones he taught us did work. That was confirmed in 1990, when Mert was awarded the Nobel Prize for economics.

Since I did the degree, the theories have been modified. But over the years that I've been a financial writer in the US, Australia and New Zealand, I've watched how the basic ideas work over and over again, in rising and falling markets. These aren't just ideas for how things are now; they are 'truths' about money. Learn them and stick to them through thick and thin – especially thin – and you will come out ahead.

Rule 1: Spread your risk

We've already talked about diversification a couple of times. Once was in Step 4: 'Join the best KiwiSaver fund for you', when we looked at investing not just in New Zealand but around the world. And the other time was in Step 5: 'Boost your saving painlessly', when I said that if you invest in rental property when you already own your home, that's a worry because you've got heaps tied up in property. But diversification applies much more broadly than that – in fact to pretty much every aspect of investing.

Diversification has been called 'the only free lunch'. Generally, in finance 'there's no such thing as a free lunch'. For example, you can't get higher returns without taking higher risk. However, with diversification you can reduce risk without reducing your average return. How come?

Maths alert! Let's say the average return on shares is 10%. (That's rather high, but it keeps the maths easy.) If you invest in one company, the return might be anything from minus 50% to plus 70%. That averages out at 10% (halfway between minus 50 and plus 70).

But if you invest in many companies, some will do well while others will do badly, so their returns will tend to offset one another. The range of returns on the whole portfolio of shares might be minus 20% to plus 40%.

The average is still 10% (halfway between minus 20 and plus 40), but you've reduced the volatility of your returns. Sure, you miss out on the chance to get 70%, but you also miss out on minus 50%. Most people like that trade-off.

Main point: If you own lots of shares you won't get the big highs or lows you can get with just one or two shares. You get a smoother ride.

Critics of diversification make comments like, 'Why would you want to spread your risk over lots of investments, including some bad ones? Just find a few good ones and stick with them.'

Just?

Sticking with shares for the moment, I reckon it's impossible to work out in advance which shares are good investments.

Why? Because it's not about the quality of the company – which can quite easily be established – it's about whether it's underpriced, so you can make a good gain on it.

Prospects for a retirement village company might look great, with so many baby boomers retiring. But if everyone realises that and therefore pushes the share price up too far, the shares will be bad investments. Benjamin Graham, an American economist and author, has observed, 'A great company is not a great investment if you pay too much for the stock.'

So how do you find underpriced shares? As I explained earlier (Step 4: 'Join the best KiwiSaver fund for you'), if an expert is the first to realise a share price will rise, he or she will make money from that info, by buying fast. But their very purchase will push up the price. The demand for that share has risen. So those following on behind won't profit from the price rise.

With lots of experts out there hoping to be first with the information, the chances that you, as a non-expert, will frequently pick which shares are going to rise fast is next to nil – unless you happen to know something juicy about the company where you or your neighbour works. But that's 'insider information', and it's illegal to trade on that. Don't try! If you're caught – and people do get caught – you will be in serious trouble.

In the absence of illegal insider info, you will still sometimes do well with your shares. Everyone is lucky sometimes. If you have several shares, some are bound to do well. Also, share markets trend upwards over time, so most shares rise.

But notice I said 'several' shares. That's the point here. You can't foresee which shares will zoom up, so diversify – hold lots of shares. Ten is good, 20 is better. As John Bogle, founder of huge index fund company Vanguard, puts it, 'Don't look for the needle in the haystack, just buy the haystack!'

The stock picking game

Earlier I mentioned that I taught a financial literacy course at the University of Auckland for five years, from 2009 to 2013. When I first planned the course, I realised that most of the students, fresh out of high school, wouldn't know much about the share market. How could I give them an idea of what a share was? Out of that question was born the Stock Picking Game.

At the start of the course, I gave the students one-page summaries from a stockbroker about 25 New Zealand shares. Each student had to choose a share they thought would perform well over the 14 weeks of the course. I also assigned each student another share. Then I divided the 25 shares into five 'portfolios', or groups of shares, and each student was assigned to a portfolio.

So, at the beginning, each student had: their chosen share, my chosen share for them, and a portfolio of five shares. Then we set it all aside until the end of the course.

Before I go any further, many of you will be saying, 'Hang on a minute. You've been telling us shares are a ten-year-plus investment. Now you've got students "investing" for 14 weeks!' Good point – a point I made repeatedly to the students. And, if I'm honest, I would have preferred it if the NZ share market had fallen during those 14 weeks, to underline how risky short-term investing can be.

No such luck – except in 2010, when 16 out of the 25 shares lost value, even after including dividends. In the other four years, the average return (including dividends) ranged from 6% to 15% – very healthy returns for just three months.

Thank goodness in most years I could refer back to unhappy 2010! And in every year there were several shares that lost value, so that helped.

But on we went. There was lots else for the students to learn. Some of the lessons:

Most students were lousy stock pickers. In 2011, for example, the most popular share was Fletcher Building, probably because students expected it to benefit from the recent Christchurch earthquakes. But in the 14 weeks, its performance ranked 20th out of 25. And the second most popular, Air New Zealand, came dead last. Meanwhile, the top-performing share, NZX, which was chosen by just three students out of 400, produced an astonishing best return of 55% in just three months.

Then in 2013 the third to last share in popularity, Xero, came top with an even more astonishing return of 70%.

Of course, the quality of the student choices wasn't always that bad. But most years the most popular shares tended to perform worse than the least popular ones.

Information affects share prices more or less immediately, and amateurs can't benefit from it after that. The popularity of Fletcher Building – because of the earthquakes – illustrates that. By the time the students were picking their stock, in March 2011, the experts had long since calculated how much that company was likely to benefit from the quakes rebuild. That information had already pushed up the share price.

Don't judge a share by its short-term return. Despite the fact that the students 'invested' for only three months, we also looked at longer-term performances of the shares. In 2011, for instance, while Fletcher Building and Air New Zealand did poorly over the three months, Air New Zealand had gained nearly 13% a year over the previous ten years. And Fletcher Building had averaged more than 20%. Their recent performances were far from typical.

A single share can be very volatile. NZX, top performer in both 2009 and 2011, came 22nd out of 25 in the year in between. Mainfreight, top in 2010, came dead last in 2013. And F&P Appliances, top in 2012, had come 20th out of 25 in 2010.

Perhaps most importantly – *diversification smooths out the ride*. When we looked at the portfolios of five shares, it showed how 'owning' more than a single share reduces the highs and lows.

In 2011, for example, the return on one share was minus 14% while on another it was plus 55%. But on the portfolios, the range was much smaller. The worst portfolio's return was plus 1% while the best one got plus 22%. The same thing happened every other year, and of course it always will; the highs and lows are watered down.

Footnote: The students didn't feel so bad about being lousy stock pickers after I told them about Lusha, the Russian circus chimp. Lusha was given the choice of 30 cubes, each with the name of a company on it. She chose eight.

A year later, her 'portfolio' – which included banks and mining companies – had grown a truly impressive three-fold. Lusha had done better than 94% of Russia's investment funds, according to Moscow TV.

Other stories tell of people throwing darts at newspaper stock price tables, buying whatever stocks the darts land on, and beating most of the experts.

What about diversifying property?

The property market is more varied. While one Air New Zealand share is the same as another, every property is unique. That makes it harder for the market to be as 'efficient' – which means the price reflects the information everybody has. There will be property bargains out there.

Still, if you're buying property as an investment rather than as a home, and you want to get those bargains, you will have to compete with people who buy and sell property for a living. They have become expert at spotting, for example, a house that can be cheaply tarted up for resale, or an office block in an area where demand for office space will grow.

I know more than one person who has felt confident they can pick bargain properties, only to be deeply disappointed. Again, it pays to diversify – which in the case of property means buying several or investing in a fund that owns lots of properties.

Managed funds

You really need, say, $100,000 to buy a wide range of shares or bonds. And to buy a range of properties, you need more. Most of us aren't in a position to do that.

That's where managed funds – in KiwiSaver and outside it – come into their own. As we looked at earlier (Step 4: 'Join the best KiwiSaver fund for you'), the lower-risk funds hold mainly cash and bonds and the higher-risk ones hold mainly shares and property.

The point here is that they hold *lots of different* bonds or shares or properties, in various industries and locations. If some of a fund's investments do badly, others do well.

Bank term deposits

Diversification applies here, too. If you have money to tie up for, say, three years, you might have the choice of:

- six-month term deposits paying 4%; or
- two-year term deposits paying 5%.

The two-year ones look better. But what if interest rates rise within the next year and you're stuck with what now looks like a low rate? On the other hand, if you go with the six-month option and interest rates fall, you'll be sorry you didn't grab the 5% rate.

Nobody is particularly good at predicting interest rates. The answer is to put half your money in each. Looking back later, you'll be glad that at least half your money was in the right place.

Owning lots of different types of assets

While it's good to own many different shares or different properties or whatever, it also reduces your risk to invest in

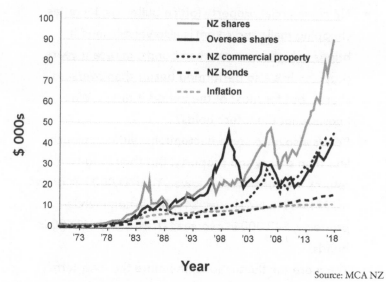

Figure 12: Different assets take different paths
Value of $1,000 invested in 1973 (after tax)

Source: MCA NZ

Technical stuff: This doesn't include costs of investing, such as brokerage or fees. That would reduce returns quite a lot over a long period. On the other hand, this graph assumes you are taxed at the top PIR rate of 28% (income over $48,000). If you were on a lower income, returns would be higher because your tax would be lower. Shares include dividends and NZ shares include imputation credits. NZ commercial property includes rental income.

different types of assets. I'm not talking here about money you expect to spend in the next year or two or three. It's best to keep that in bank term deposits. But beyond that, a mix is best. When one type of assets does badly another is likely to do well and compensate.

Shares include dividends, and NZ shares include imputation credits. NZ commercial property includes rental income.

Points to notice about Figure 12:

- The value of all assets rises over time. But there are periods when the rise of one would offset the fall of another – if you have invested in both.
- While you get a rougher ride in NZ and overseas shares, for most of the period they bring in the highest returns.
- NZ commercial property (office buildings, factories, shopping malls and so on) is also volatile, and it brings in higher returns than bonds. In recent years, property has also performed better than overseas shares, but for most of the period it didn't. Who knows what the future holds?
- Bonds also have some fluctuations, although much less than shares and property. But their long-term returns are considerably lower. Your $1,000 has grown to: $91,000 in NZ shares; $46,000 in commercial property; $43,000 in overseas shares; and $17,000 in bonds.
- The more the fluctuations, the more the long-term growth.

True tale: Not such a good mix

In New Zealand's version of the global financial crisis of 2007–08, finance companies were hit worst. Enticed by high interest rates, people had put large deposits with companies that made much riskier investments than they let on.

A financial regulator friend says: 'We wanted to find out what people were doing investing in these things. It turned out they had gone to a financial planner, often an ex-insurance agent who had no idea. But the agents got trips around the world from the finance companies.

'The planners thought that being in five or six finance companies was a diversified portfolio. They were really junk bonds. A good portfolio would have no more than 5% or 6% of those, and most would have none.

'People were seduced by the interest rates they saw in the paper every day. In the global financial crisis they lost everything.'

> **Moral:** Don't put all your investments in one type of asset.

So how do you get a good spread of different types of assets?

To do this easily, turn to good old managed funds again. A balanced fund, for instance, typically holds several different types of assets.

Rule 2: Largely ignore past performance

Firstly, why did I say 'largely' in the heading? There are some things we can learn by looking at how investments have performed in the past. In the KiwiSaver step we noted that:

- A consistently bad investment is probably best avoided.
- Past performance, especially over many years, gives you an idea of the *range* of returns you might experience in the future.

But please don't expect an investment that has done well – or badly – in the past year to continue to do well or badly. In sports and the arts, whoever did well last year is quite likely to do well again this year. But not in investing. Ads for investments quite often say something like 'Past performance is not a guide to future performance', but many people ignore that. Don't!

Figure 13 shows that returns on assets can change abruptly from year to year. Some points to note:

- Every type of asset, except cash, was best in at least one year and worst in at least one year.
- While sometimes there were runs – where the same asset was best or worst for two or three years – quite often an asset flipped from being best to worst, or vice versa, within a year or two.
- The highest returns were in property or shares – but so were the lowest returns. These are higher-risk investments.
- A return of 7% was the worst in 2005 but the best in 2010. Some years are just much better than others for all assets.

Clearly, past performance is rarely repeated, except in cash – and even in cash there was a huge change between 2008 and 2009.

Figure 13: Which asset did best – and worst?

Percentage returns on assets over 10 years. Numbers in
underlined italics show the worst performing asset that year.
Numbers in **bold** show the best performing asset that year.

Year	Cash	NZ bonds	Overseas bonds	Commercial property	NZ shares	Overseas shares
2005	7	_7_	9	**20**	11	16
2006	8	_4_	6	**25**	22	16
2007	9	4	**9**	_-4_	3	0
2008	9	**16**	15	-21	_-32_	-22
2009	3	_2_	4	12	**21**	4
2010	3	**7**	_2_	3	4	7
2011	3	**13**	8	11	-1	_-14_
2012	_3_	5	7	21	**27**	10
2013	3	_-2_	3	4	18	**27**
2014	_3_	8	12	**24**	19	11
2015	_3_	5	5	14	**15**	13
2016	_3_	3	6	3	**10**	6
2017	_2_	5	3	13	**24**	20

Source: MCA NZ

The Economist magazine didn't look at just 13 years – like
our table – but the whole of last century. What, they asked,
would happen to an investor who started out with $1 in
1900 and had perfect foresight? On every 1 January she
moved her money into the type of asset that was going to
perform best in the coming year. By the year 2000 she – or

perhaps it would be her grandchild by then – would have $1,300,000,000,000,000. Extraordinary!

But of course she doesn't have that foresight, so she settles instead for moving each January to the asset that did best in the *previous* year. What does she end up with in 2000? $290.

You get similar results if you look at which shares or managed funds performed best – or pretty much any other investment.

The fact that returns quite often swing from great to horrid, or back the other way, is no accident. In a share, for example, returns might soar as investors become excited and rush in. At some point, they start to realise some investors have overdone it, and the price can plunge quite suddenly.

Or the reverse. There's been a share market crash. But a few days or weeks later, people start to realise that prices have simply dropped too far, and there are bargains to be had. If enough people think that, share prices can climb back surprisingly fast.

An interesting example of big swings back and forth can be found in the performance of different share markets around the world. For this exercise, I looked at the biggest markets plus Australia and New Zealand. The list is: Australia, Canada, China, France, Germany, India, Italy, Japan, New Zealand, the UK and the US.

Figure 14 shows that back in 1985, Italy was the best performing market, with a return of 103%, which means share values more than doubled in a single year. Meanwhile, Japan did worst that year – with a highly respectable 15%. In the mid 1980s, share markets around the world were going nuts.

That continued into 1986, when New Zealand topped all the markets. Our 111% is the highest of any return in the table.

Figure 14: Every dog has its day

Different share markets' performance over 33 years

Year	Best country	Return %	Worst country	Return %
1985	Italy	103	Japan	15
1986	*New Zealand*	111	Germany	7
1987	Japan	9	*New Zealand*	− 44
1988	France	57	New Zealand	1
1989	Germany	40	New Zealand	16
1990	US	− 2	Japan	− 40
1991	Australia	38	Japan	0
1992	UK	19	Japan	− 21
1993	Italy	50	US	10
1994	*India*	10	China	− 46
1995	US	38	*India*	− 23
1996	*China*	38	Japan	− 5
1997	Italy	59	*China*	− 25
1998	Italy	43	China	− 42
1999	India	92	Australia	11
2000	Canada	9	China	− 30
2001	New Zealand	13	China	− 25
2002	India	8	Germany	− 43
2003	*China*	87	*Australia*	13
2004	*Australia*	27	*China*	2
2005	*Japan*	45	US	6
2006	China	83	*Japan*	7
2007	China	67	Japan	− 10
2008	UK	− 28	*India*	− 56
2009	*India*	94	Japan	9
2010	Germany	17	Italy	− 8
2011	US	2	India	− 25
2012	Germany	30	Canada	8
2013	Japan	55	China	4
2014	India	26	UK	1
2015	New Zealand	15	*Canada*	− 8
2016	*Canada*	21	Italy	− 7
2017	China	55	*Canada*	4

Source: MCA NZ

But look what happened the following year. Our minus 44% is the second worst in the whole table. From a mighty height, the local market plummeted. And we were also worst for the next two years.

The numbers show that the New Zealand share market can be particularly volatile. All the more reason to have a fair chunk of your investments overseas.

Some other things to note about Figure 14:

- Firstly, can you spot why I've put some countries in bold? (To give you a minute to work it out, I'll answer that in our fourth bullet point.)
- Almost every share market was the best performer at least once and the worst performer at least once.
- Some years are so much better than others for everyone. Take a look at 2008, the year of the global financial crisis. The best anyone could do was *minus* 28% in the UK, while Indian shares dropped 56%. That means that they more than halved.
- Why the italics? It's when a country moved from either best one year to worst the next, or the opposite. It happened fairly often, when a share market simply dropped or rose too much, and returned to sanity the following year. Check out 2003 and 2004, when China and Australia swapped places. And what about Canada's recent run!
- Just to confuse us, there are also periods when a market will do particularly well or badly for two or three years in a row.

What about share funds? Do the good performers stay good?

We looked at this earlier (Step 4: 'Join the best KiwiSaver fund for you'), where we found that most active share funds (remember them – as opposed to index funds?) don't keep performing well year after year.

Other research has much the same findings for all share funds, which is why I say 'Go with the low-fee funds'. Returns change, but low fees tend to stay low.

Against the flow

The fact that top performers can later plunge, and bottom performers later soar, has led some investors to take an interest in what's called *contrarian investing* – moving your money into what's performed *badly* lately. There are even contrarian funds in the US and elsewhere that invest not only in whatever is unpopular in shares but also bonds, currencies, commodities, property and so on – anything where values move up and down.

Contrarian investors tend to do better than other frequent traders. But sometimes they land up in disastrous investments that are on their way to being worth zero. They get it wrong often enough that it's better to just select the best long-term investments for you and hold them.

True tale: Quite contrary

A while back I received an interesting letter from a reader of my *Weekend Herald* Q&A column. 'I think I need help!' he wrote. 'I'm not a negative kind of person at all, but every time the market drops for something, I am ready to buy.

'I see bargains when share prices drop. I feel like I am getting a bargain, as if the share is on sale. Have I stumbled on the recipe for wealth or am I crazy? Note – I only use spare cash. I am not so crazy that I would do this with my retirement savings!'

This man – a good example of a contrarian investor – is miles ahead of most people. The common reaction to a market fall is to sell, not buy. But the market as a whole always recovers. Companies keep selling goods and services. Most of them make a profit most of the time, and their share prices reflect that.

So if you buy a range of shares when prices are low, you should do better than all the investors who buy only in rising markets. But it's still not the best strategy. You're still just guessing what markets will do.

> **Moral:** If you must time markets, be contrarian. But, as I told this man, it's better still to forget market timing and drip-feed, which leads us to our next rule.

Rule 3: Don't try to time markets

'Is now the time to buy?' or 'Should I be selling now?' People often ask these questions after watching the share or property market rise or fall fast.

But by the time you've asked, it's probably too late. The price has already moved. And it's quite likely, in fact, that its next move will be in the *opposite* direction because the gain or drop was just too big.

Paul Samuelson, the first American to win the Nobel Prize in economics (and author of the economics textbook many of my generation used), once said, 'The stock market has forecast nine of the last five recessions.' In other words, downturns often seemed to be on the way, but they didn't come.

And many stock market gurus, who became famous because they predicted a big rise or fall, have since wrecked their reputations. Morgan Stanley – a global financial services firm that would actually benefit from people moving their money in and out of markets – has commented on a study that tracked more than 4,500 forecasts by 28 self-described market timers, between 2000 and 2012. Only ten accurately predicted share returns more than half the time, 'and none were able to predict accurately enough to outperform the market'.

Says Morgan Stanley: 'As history has shown repeatedly, market timing is a losing game ... Volumes of research critical of the practice have been written, and some of the greatest investment minds – William Sharpe, a Nobel laureate, Benjamin Graham, considered the father of value investing and John Bogle, founder of The Vanguard Group – have all counselled against it.'

Market timers often pull right out of share markets for a while – leaving after prices have plunged and coming back in after the market has risen. They take the falls and miss the rises. That can be a very expensive habit.

Let's say you had $10,000 to invest in US shares at the end of 2001. If you had just left the money there, you would have had nearly $28,700 by the end of 2016 – a respectable average return of 7.3% a year.

But if you were in and out of the market and happened to miss:

- The best ten days – just ten days out of 15 years – your investment would have been worth $14,700. That's just over half!
- The 20 best days, your $10,000 would have ended up as $9,600. Your investment went backwards.

All the action happens, it seems, in short spurts. Another long-term study found that there's an average of just three days a year when nearly all the share growth occurs.

The above research is a bit silly in a way. Nobody would be that unlucky. Also, if you were out of the market a lot you'd probably also miss some of the worst days. But share markets trend upwards, so there are more good days than bad.

How to invest in up and down markets

The best and easiest way is to drip-feed your money in – the same amount every week or month – *regardless* of what markets are doing. Back in Step 5: 'Boost your saving painlessly', we talked about how this is difficult to do with property. But it's easy with managed funds, including KiwiSaver.

Most people in KiwiSaver drip-feed into their account without even thinking about it. That includes all employees and others who have set up automatic payments into their account. You can do the same thing with many other managed funds, and it's a great idea.

The magic of regular saving

If you're making regular deposits of the same amount into any investment where the balance goes up and down – such as a KiwiSaver or non-KiwiSaver fund that includes shares, property or bonds – you'll benefit from something called *dollar cost averaging.* It's a confusing name – and in fact the whole concept is confusing for some people. If you can't follow this, don't worry. It works regardless of whether you know how it's happening!

But let's try to appreciate it.

When you invest in almost all funds, you buy what are called units. What follows also applies if you are buying individual shares, but we'll use units in our example.

Maths alert! This is a ridiculously oversimplified example, to keep the maths easy to follow.

We'll say you invest $1,200 a month into a fund.

For six months of the year, the units cost $12 each. So your $1,200 buys you 100 units a month. Over those six months, you've bought 6 x 100, which is 600 units.

In the other six months, units are only $8 each. With your $1,200 you buy 150 units a month. Over those six months, you've bought 6 x 150, which is 900 units.

Let's review the facts:

- The average price over the year is $10 – halfway between $12 and $8.
- You've bought 600 plus 900 units – a total of 1,500 units.
- With the average price at $10, you would expect to have paid $10 x 1,500, or $15,000.
- In fact, though, you've paid $1,200 a month x 12 months, which comes to only $14,400!
- You've saved $600.

Main point: If the price goes up and down but you keep investing the same amount each month (or week), you end up getting bargains.

How did you get so lucky?

It's quite simple really. You bought more units when they were cheaper, and fewer when they were more expensive. Furthermore, the more volatile the investment, the bigger the savings.

In some ways, then, a downturn is good news for regular contributors. It means you buy at cheap prices. You just need faith that the markets will rise again – and they will!

What if you have a lump sum to invest?

Perhaps you have an inheritance, or you've sold the bach or some other large asset?

Drip-feeding portions over time is still a good idea, so you don't end up putting the lot into, say, a share fund, only to see the share market drop soon afterwards. That would be seriously discouraging. On the other hand, if you drip-feed for too long, the rest of the money is probably sitting in a bank term deposit in the meantime, earning a rather low return.

A good compromise is to do it monthly over a year. Or put a third in now, a third in after six months and a third in after 12 months.

It's similar, actually, if you want to move some money from one country to another. Forecasting foreign exchange rates is just as fruitless as forecasting other market movements. So it works best to move it in a few chunks rather than all at once.

Resist temptation

Market timers tend to trade frequently. So do other people who simply like trading. There's nothing inherently wrong with frequent trading, but you will nearly always end up worse off.

Your uncle might argue with that. He's done really well by trading shares over the years. What he probably doesn't realise is how much better he could have done.

One study looked at US investments between 1991 and 2010. The S&P500, an index that covers basically the biggest 500 US companies listed on the stock market, rose an average of 7.7% a year in that period – despite the global financial crisis in 2007–08. How did the average share fund investor do over that period? They got an average return of just 2.6%.

That makes a huge difference. If our investor had put $10,000 into an S&P500 index fund and left it there over the 20 years, it would have grown to $44,000. But if he or she had been a typical investor, it would have grown to just $16,700 – not much more than one-third of $44,000.

A more recent study, in 2017, found that over the previous 30 years, the S&P500 grew by 10.2% a year. But the average investor in share funds saw 4.0% growth.

Why do traders do worse? For one thing, impatience. The data 'strongly suggests that investors lack the patience and long-term vision to stay invested in any one fund for much more than four years,' says Lance Roberts, writing in the *Wall Street Journal*. 'Jumping into and out of investments every few years is not a prudent strategy because investors are simply unable to correctly time when to make such moves.'

But also there are trading costs – brokerage, tax, commissions and legal fees. Tax? Well yes. New Zealand has a rather wobbly law about tax on investment gains. Many more people probably should be paying than do. However, that looks quite likely to change soon. Anyway, in the meantime, frequent traders are much more likely to end up actually paying the tax.

And over 20 or 30 years, if you pay 30% tax on your gains you're likely to end up with about half of what you would have had if you had left the same money in an investment without trading. If you pay 33% tax, it's even worse. Warren Buffett is happy sitting on the sidelines: 'I never attempt to make money on the stock market. I buy on the assumption that they could close the market the next day and not reopen it for ten years.'

There's not so much research on property, probably because every property is different. But the comments of Wellingtonian Mark Dunajtschik, 82 – former concentration camp prisoner and now property developer who in 2017 donated $50 million for a children's hospital in Wellington – are interesting.

'I am absolutely convinced that time is the hardest worker for property investment,' he says. 'Bob Jones said that ... all property developers go broke and the only exception he knows is that bugger Mark Dunajtschik, and the reason he doesn't go broke is because he keeps his property.'

> **Key message:** Investing is one of the few human endeavours where doing less is better.

True tale: Amazing Grace

When Grace Groner, of the Chicago suburb of Lake Forest, died in 2010 at age 100, most people were astonished that her estate was worth $7 million.

'She got her clothes from rummage sales,' reported the *Chicago Tribune*. 'She walked everywhere rather than buy a car. And her one-bedroom house in Lake Forest held little more than a few plain pieces of furniture, some mismatched dishes and a hulking TV set that appeared left over from the Johnson administration.'

Where had the money come from? 'In 1935, she bought three $60 shares of specially issued Abbott stock and never sold them. The shares split many times over the next seven decades, and Groner reinvested the dividends,' said the *Tribune*.

She left the money to a local college so that students could take up internships and study-abroad programs.

> **Moral:** It's often best to buy and hold shares, rather than trading. We should note, though, that Grace could have reduced her risk by buying shares in more than one company. She got lucky!

When you *should* move your money or sell

The basic rule is to make these moves because of things going on in your life, as opposed to things going on in the markets.

Some examples of when you should move or sell:

- When you get within a few years of spending the money – for example, if you're in KiwiSaver you might be planning to buy a first home or spend the money in retirement. You don't want to find that right before you take out your money the market has plunged. If you've gradually moved to a low-risk fund a couple of years earlier this won't happen.
- If you've realised you're in a riskier fund than you can cope with. But if you move for this reason, don't switch back later!

- If you've realised you would prefer to take on more risk – knowing you'll be okay with the ups and downs and you want higher long-term growth.
- The fund turns out to have high fees, or to offer poor customer service.

If you want to move to a different fund, but with the same provider – in or out of KiwiSaver – it should be easy and in most cases fee-free. Often you'll be able to make the move online.

Rebalancing

Another reason to move money is *rebalancing*. Let's say you've decided that the best mix for you is to have half your money in a balanced fund and the other half in a riskier share fund. Over time, though, they won't stay half and half. One fund will grow more than the other, or in a downturn one will fall less than the other.

If you like the 50:50 split, you should review your investments, say, every three years.

An easy way to fix an imbalance is to make all new deposits into the fund that's fallen behind. But if you're not depositing much, or the imbalance has got bad, you may want to move some money from one fund to the other.

Don't go all the way back to 50:50 though. Keep in mind that the next market move might take you there anyway. As long as you hover fairly close to 50:50, that's fine. But if you don't rebalance at all, your 50:50 split can get seriously out of whack over the years.

A financial adviser I know says his clients often baulk at rebalancing, which is hardly surprising. After all, they're moving funds from a recently successful investment to a less successful one.

He finds it helps to remind them that they're buying cheaply in the less successful investment. And in any case, it may turn out to be the better investment in future.

A reminder: Whether you're moving money to rebalance or for another reason, if a large amount is involved it's usually better to move it gradually. As we've said before, you don't want to move all your money into a fund right before it plunges.

Rule 4: Never be forced to sell

There's not a lot to say about this rule, but that doesn't make it any less important.

We've talked earlier about how people who are forced to sell rental property may well find they have to sell right when house prices are low. The same thing can happen with shares or other investments – especially if you take high risks, or borrow to invest and therefore have to make interest payments.

It's a really good idea to think through a worst case scenario before you take on a riskier investment. Include such events as losing your job or losing another source of income. How would you cope?

If you have lots of savings or family who could help you out in a crunch, that's fine. But if not, take care. It's when people are forced to sell that the horrible situations arise.

Remember – risky investments are for the long term. Don't have the term cut short against your will.

The longer the term, the less the risk

Some US research shows how being in a higher-risk investment is much less risky over a long period. Investment service company Charles Schwab looked at returns on shares in the S&P500 index. It found that between 1926 and 2011 – a period that included really good and really bad times in the markets – the range of returns on shares narrowed markedly, depending on how long you held them.

- Over single years, the returns ranged from minus 43% to plus 54%.
- Over five-year periods, they ranged from minus 13% to plus 29%.
- Over ten-year periods, they ranged from minus 1% to plus 20%.
- Over 20-year periods, they ranged from plus 3% to plus 18%.

The longer you held the shares, the less dramatic the high returns, but also the less dramatic the low returns.

Over any ten-year period, the worst that happened was a 1% loss, and in the vast majority of the ten-year periods there was a healthy gain, ranging up to 20%. And there was never a loss over any 20-year period.

Rule 5: Sit back and relax

You've had enough rules by now: diversify, don't chase returns, don't time markets, don't be forced to sell. And earlier on you were warned not to borrow too much. But here comes the easiest rule of all:

- Get yourself set up – which might simply mean getting into the right KiwiSaver fund for you, but might also include other investments.
- Test that you can cope with the bad times. If you're in higher-risk investments – in or out of KiwiSaver – imagine how you would feel if your balance halved. If you would move to a lower-risk investment, do so now, rather than when the markets have plunged and you're turning losses on paper into actual losses. But if you would stick it out, that's great. A good diversified investment will always come right in time.
- Do little else. Sure, check every now and then whether you need to rebalance, or move money as you get closer to spending time. But that's all. Economist Paul Samuelson has put it this way: 'Investing should be more like watching paint dry or watching grass grow. if you want excitement, take $800 and go to Las Vegas.'

True tale: What not to do

A KiwiSaver provider tells me that a member of his scheme contacted him complaining because the return on his KiwiSaver account was minus 5% for the year ending 31 March 2017. I would have complained, too. That was a year when the markets were humming along nicely, so what's with this loss?

The provider was equally puzzled, until he checked the man's track record. It turns out he was a particularly diligent investor.

Every month he had looked at the returns on all of the provider's KiwiSaver funds, and moved his money to the fund that had performed best in the previous month. He had done that *11* times in the year!

If he had stayed in his original balanced fund, his return would have been a highly respectable 9.2%.

> **Moral:** Get into the right investments and leave them alone.

The psychology of investing

Why do so many people find it hard to keep their hands off their investments or make other wealth-destroying moves?

Lots of research has looked at how our emotions affect the ways we invest. The following are some of the little games we get up to – to our financial cost. If you're aware of them, you can often overcome them, or at least make allowances for them.

Loss aversion

We have stronger *negative* feelings about loss than we have *positive* feelings about gain.

Nobel Prize winner Daniel Kahneman, one of the first to write about how psychology affects investing, observed in his book *'Thinking, Fast and Slow'* that 'Closely following daily [stock market] fluctuations is a losing proposition, because the pain of the frequent small losses exceeds the pleasure of the equally frequent small gains.'

Looking backwards

We become absorbed in how much we paid for something, possibly years ago. Often this means we won't sell an investment simply because we refuse to sell at a loss.

What's past is past. We need to ask ourselves if an investment is right for us *now*, and get rid of it if it's not.

Herding

This is common – the tendency to do what other people are doing, whether it be buying or selling certain assets. Usually, by the time we take action, the good price has gone – if it ever was really a good investment in the first place.

Herding is comforting. If you lose and everyone else does, too, it doesn't seem so bad. But a loss is still a loss. As we've observed, contrarian investors, who do the opposite of nearly everyone else, tend to do somewhat better than those following the mainstream.

Expecting the same market conditions to continue

This is particularly true if a market has been growing for several years. Investors forget the earlier down times, and think the good times will roll on forever. Or they think low mortgage interest rates will continue forever.

Sticking with the status quo

Our investments might no longer be suitable for us, but we don't get around to changing them.

Let's say your investments total $100,000. It's a great idea to every now and then write down how you would invest that $100,000 if you were given it today. Then look into switching to those investments.

Responding to how something is presented

Which do you prefer: an investment that gains value nine years out of ten or an investment that loses value one year in ten? Think about it!

Letting a name mislead you

When a fund manager changed the name of a fund from 'Junk Bonds' to 'High-Yield Bonds' the investments didn't change. They were high-risk and high-return. But a lot more people invested.

Emotional attachment

You inherited the shares from Grandpa, so you feel you have to stick with them. But would Grandpa really want you to do that, when you could be using the money in a much better way?

Being overwhelmed with information

These days, we don't get too little info on potential investments, but too much. It's hard to know what to take notice of.

That can lead to doing nothing. The stack of documents sits on your kitchen bench for weeks, until it becomes 'just part of the furniture'. Can't decide? Choose a couple of good investments, split your money between them, and get on with it.

Overconfidence

A little early success can be a dangerous thing. You buy a share and then its price zooms up, or you buy a rental property and then prices soar. It's too easy to tell yourself you have the knack, and invest a whole lot more – only to see your luck turn against you.

True tale: On the bandwagon

A member of a wealthy New Zealand family came to his stockbroker in mid 1987, when the share market was in the midst of probably its maddest boom ever. He proudly showed the broker his portfolio of shares. They included about $20 million in the shares everyone else was in – Equiticorp, Chase, Judge Corp, Euronational and so on.

'We were quite risk averse,' says the broker. 'We suggested he get out. But he ignored us. Each day the market was rising three or four per cent and he wanted to be part of it. On the day of the crash, he said, "You were right," and gave us orders to sell.'

At least the shares were sold while they were still worth something. 'Most of those companies didn't exist six months or a year later,' says the broker. 'They'd gone.' But still, the investor had lost heaps – as did many other share investors less able to weather that storm.

Moral: Don't follow the crowds when you invest.

Vive la différence: how men and women invest

The first thing to say here is that there are many exceptions to the 'rules'. However, I'm including this because it might draw your attention to weaknesses in the way you invest. Also, it's interesting.

Let's start with a couple of quizzes. The first is about gender and goal setting:

Which gender is more likely to achieve their goals if:

1. They set a specific rather than vague goal?
2. They told friends and family about it at the start?
3. They were encouraged not to give up if they lapsed – for example, they went on a chocolate binge when on a diet?
4. They focused on rewards associated with achieving the goal?

Answers in a minute.

Next we have a Colmar Brunton survey, in which they asked people: 'Which of the following is most important to you when making an investment decision?' There were strong gender biases in the answers to 2, 3 and 4. Can you guess them?

1. Being able to access money whenever you want.
2. Maintaining all the money originally invested.
3. Earning a reliable return – value of investment increases steadily.
4. Earning the best return overall – even if investment value changes over time.
5. Doubling your money in ten years.

Answers: On gender and goal setting, women are more likely to achieve their goals if they do 2 and 3, and men are more likely to succeed if they do 1 and 4, according to www.quirkology.com/UK.

In the survey, women were more likely to say 2, and men were more likely to say 3 or 4. (Men and women were about equally likely to say 1 or 5.)

Much other research has come up with two basic gender differences in investment style: men are more likely to prefer higher-risk investments; and men trade more.

We'll look at risk first.

While higher-risk investing tends to bring in higher returns, sometimes men go for too much risk. Women, on the other hand, tend to take too little risk.

In an ANZ survey, people were asked, 'Are you confident you'll reach your retirement savings goal?' About 55% of men said yes, but only 41% of women said yes. This is probably partly because women are more likely to take time out from paid work and are paid less, but it's probably also because women are more likely to be in investments with lower returns.

Also, they might simply take less interest. Research by the Financial Markets Authority found young women 'are the least engaged with their KiwiSaver materials and they are least likely to take action' to get more out of KiwiSaver.

Conclusion: Women should think hard about whether they should increase their investment risk. And men should consider reducing their risk – by diversifying; using higher-risk investments only for the long haul; and keeping their borrowing low (men tend to have higher debt).

On trading frequency, research shows that women tend to buy and hold investments, while men are more likely to trade – usually to their detriment, as explained above.

An example of men's counter-productive trading: a study of 2.7 million investors during the global financial crisis in 2007–08 found that men were much more likely than women to sell their shares at market lows.

Why do men trade more frequently? Studies have found that frequent traders tend to believe they are the exception; they will do well – although most of them don't.

Should men be more confident with their money than women? Hard to say. Some research suggests men know more than women about finance, but other research finds they are about equal. Even if men do know more, they don't know enough to trade successfully over time! It's probably significant to note here that more compulsive gamblers are male than female.

What explains the gender differences?

If you read through the literature on this, a few ideas keep popping up. Women, some research shows, are more likely to seek financial help and advice. They're more patient, and more likely to set goals. That could explain why they're less likely to trade impulsively.

Men tend to be more competitive, and to see money as a way of keeping score.

If these differences ring true for you and your partner – regardless of who has which characteristics – it's probably a good idea for you to make financial decisions together. Each of you can benefit from the other's strengths, and counteract the other's flaws! But if you can't agree on a strategy, maybe you could each be in charge of 50% of your investments, so you have a range of risks and styles.

Who gets scammed?

There are gender patterns in scam victims.

Australian research on 80 telemarketing scams found that 90% of the victims were men.

And the Commission for Financial Capability says that UK research 'found that older, wealthier, risk-taking men are the most likely targets for "share fraud", when worthless or unsellable company shares are on offer. Women are more affected by "recovery fraud", when scammers offer to recover funds or a lost investment in exchange for a fee.'

Interestingly, it adds, 'The UK study demonstrated that the more financially sophisticated a person is, the more likely they are to be victimised, since fraudsters prey on investors' overconfidence.'

Many people of both genders don't like to tell others that they are victims. So scams are more widespread than we realise.

Step 6 check

Have you:

- ❏ Taken steps to spread your risk – over different assets and by holding lots of investments in each type of asset?
- ❏ Stopped taking notice of which investments did best last year or last decade?
- ❏ Given up on market timing and trading, and instead set up regular investments?
- ❏ Made sure you won't be forced to sell?
- ❏ Considered how psychology and gender might be hurting your investing?

Reward

Chocolates, cheese or flowers; or a 'me day' with a walk, book, time with family, being creative; or donating to a charity, or anything else that makes you smile.

What's next? How will it be for you when your working days are over?

Step 7

HEAD CONFIDENTLY TOWARDS RETIREMENT – AND THROUGH IT

In which we …

- Work out roughly how long you are likely to live (probably!)
- Take comfort about NZ Super
- Decide to SKI through retirement
- Set a retirement savings goal, panic, and then …
- … Look at many ways to make it easier
- Consider KiwiSaver and other investments in retirement

'Retirement?' you say (perhaps). 'That's many, many years away for me, and I've got so many other financial things to think about before then. I'm saving for retirement in KiwiSaver. That's enough on that topic for me right now, thanks.'

If that's you, that's fine. I totally understand. I've been there – although it was some time back now! So if you want to skip this step and get back to it in ten or 20 years, it will keep. Still, it mightn't be a bad idea to have a quick flick through, just to have an idea of where you might be heading when you get to your late forties or older.

Meanwhile, for everyone else – right up to centenarians and beyond – let's look at how to set up your money for retirement in an easy-to-understand and easy-to-use way.

Some critics might say my way is too simple. But there will always be 'ifs' and 'buts' and 'maybes' in retirement planning, because nobody can predict future returns. So I see no point in being highly detailed.

Here's a thought to help you on your way: Saving for your retirement doesn't just make you happy when you're retired. It also makes you more comfortable in the meantime, knowing you're planning for the time when you'll earn less money.

The big picture

Firstly, let's address perhaps the most important issue of all.

How long are you likely to live?

Of course nobody knows. You could die today. But barring accidents, we can get a rough idea of your life expectancy.

These days in New Zealand a man of 65 can expect to live – on average – until he's 84. For a woman of 65 it's until she's 87. Note, though, that life expectancy keeps rising. So if you're not yet in your sixties, the number might be several years higher by the time you get there.

In any case, those numbers are very rough. We all know many factors affect longevity. So, for a more accurate estimate of your own life expectancy at your current age, I suggest you go to the Lifespan Calculator at www.tinyurl.com/ExpectLife.

I really like this calculator. It considers all sorts of factors, such as your family history and driving record, and even whether you wear a car seatbelt. It also helps you to see how you could make changes that would increase your life expectancy. For example, if you increase how much you exercise, or eat better, reduce excess drinking, or stop smoking, you can see how each of those changes would affect your likely life span.

This calculator is American, so you have to give your height in feet and inches (which is probably not a problem for many of us older ones!). And your weight needs to be in pounds. If you know your weight only in kilograms, just Google '70 kilograms in pounds' and it will convert it for you. The same goes for height – Google '170 cms in feet and inches'.

Just for fun, I filled out the calculator as if I were an 80-year-old woman who did everything right – starting out with being a woman, given that women live longer than men! Her life expectancy is 108. For a similarly saintly man of 80, it's 104.

What to expect from NZ Super?

Earlier in this book I said, 'I'm confident there'll be reasonable NZ Super available for everyone in the decades to come.'

That's not a common view. Younger people often say they expect the pension to be slashed, if not ended, by the time they get to retirement.

Many people in the financial world are happy about that expectation, and some even foster it. They point out that our population is ageing as the baby boomers reach retirement age and beyond. The number of people working to support the number of retirees is decreasing. 'You'd better save heaps!' they say. The more subtle message is: 'Preferably in my products.'

Of course I'm not anti-saving. But it's simply not true that NZ Super is likely to be cut way back.

NZ Super cost less than 5% of our gross domestic product before tax in 2017. The average for pensions in all countries in the OECD (Organisation for Economic Co-operation and Development) is 9%. If we change nothing, NZ's cost is expected to rise to 8.4% by 2060. While the experts want to get that down, no expert is calling for drastic measures.

A few years ago I did some work with Treasury on their 'Long-term Fiscal Statement'. It sounds rather boring, but the idea is simple enough. Every few years Treasury looks at government spending and priorities over the next 40 years. And this of course includes the rising future costs of NZ Super.

It was interesting to see the different future scenarios the officials were considering. Currently, NZ Super is raised each 1 April to keep pace with rising average wages. In most years, wages rise faster than inflation, so NZ Super also grows faster than inflation.

What we could do instead, officials suggested, is link Super to inflation. That, plus gradually raising the age NZ Super starts from 65 to 67, would go a long way towards making ends meet in future.

A switch to inflation linkage would not be insignificant. While people living on just NZ Super could continue to afford the same treats and cheap 'senior' Tuesday afternoon movies, there would be a growing gap between them and working people.

Treasury officials were worried about that gap. Some were saying perhaps the annual adjustment to Super could be halfway between wage rises and inflation.

This is a million miles away from axing NZ Super altogether. And while none of us can predict what future governments will do, I believe it's far more likely they will make fairly moderate changes.

One change that seems inevitable, though, is a rise in the starting age. Similar changes are already happening in many other countries, including Australia, Denmark, Germany and the UK and US.

In late 2016, the Commission for Financial Capability recommended raising the NZ Super age in three-month increments. The change, if it were adopted, would start in 2027. People who were 55 in late 2016 would get Super at 65 years and 3 months; 54-year-olds would get it at 65 years and 6 months; and so on, until 48-year-olds and younger would get it at 67.

In 2017, the National government proposed a more gradual change, which would affect people born after June 1972.

If a change along these lines occurs, I don't think it will be a big deal. When the Super age rose a whole five years – from 60 to 65 – between 1992 and 2001, there wasn't much outcry. And given that life expectancies keep rising, anyone who starts Super at 67 will probably end up getting at least as many years of payments as current retirees get.

If you're worried about future changes to NZ Super, just remember that a growing chunk of voters will be retired. In 2018, about 20% of New Zealanders 18 and older are over 65. Fifty years later it's expected to be 35%. What's more, the elderly are more likely to vote. In the 2014 election, only 70% of people aged 18 to 24 went to the polls, but 94% of those aged 65 and over got out and voted. No government is going to trample on all those voters.

How much is NZ Super?

In 2018–19:

- Single people living alone get $463 a week before tax, or about $24,000 a year.
- A married couple, who both qualify, get $702 a week before tax, or about $36,500 a year.

In winter, from May through September, there's also a tax-free winter energy payment. Single people with no dependent children get an extra $20 a week, and couples or people with dependent children get $32 a week. Anyone who says they don't need that extra money can choose not to receive it.

NZ Super payments are made fortnightly. Apart from the winter energy payment, Super is taxed like other income.

Many older New Zealanders are largely dependent on NZ Super. In a 2017 report, 'The Material Wellbeing of NZ Households', Bryan Perry says of New Zealanders aged 65 and older: '40% of singles have virtually no other income source, 60% report less than $100 per week from non-government sources, and 75% have more than half their income from NZ Super.'

But couples over 65 are better off. 'For example only 30% of couples report less than $100 per capita per week from non-government sources – but most couples are nevertheless still highly dependent on NZ Super, with 55% having more than half their income from NZ Super.'

I hope you won't be one of those heavily dependent on Super. If you take the steps in this book, you shouldn't be.

Tip: You can apply for NZ Super up to 12 weeks before your 65th birthday, and it's a good idea to get in your application around then. It can take a little while to process, and if you turn 65 in the meantime you don't get backdated money.

Setting a retirement savings goal

Before we get going, there are two important points:

- A retirement savings goal has got to be approximate – but I'll help you make a reasonable estimate. It's helpful to have something to aim at.
- The numbers in this section might look rather daunting. But don't be discouraged. The next section is called 'Making it easier'!

As you'll see in our final step (Step ?: 'Buy a home, or sell one'), we're not automatically assuming in this book that you own a home or will ever own one. But if you decide to opt out of home ownership, you obviously need to retire with extra savings to cover the costs of your accommodation.

However, most people own their own home in retirement. The numbers: 83% of New Zealanders over 65 (excluding people in residential aged-care facilities) currently live in dwellings owned by them or their trust.

And a majority of younger New Zealanders will probably continue to buy houses and – hopefully – be mortgage-free by the time they stop working.

A 2018 BNZ survey found almost three-quarters of New Zealanders 'are confident they will pay off their mortgage before they retire or semi-retire'. Others plan to use some of their KiwiSaver savings or other investments to make the last mortgage payments, or sell their home and buy a cheaper one.

If you're a homeowner and none of those plans will work for you, you'll need to add mortgage costs to your savings goal – or take some of the steps suggested in 'Making it easier'.

Skiing through retirement

This is not about taking to the slopes. It's SKI, which stands for Spend the Kids' Inheritance!

People on lower incomes have, of course, always been unable to leave much of an inheritance. But a generation or two ago, better off people usually left something to their offspring, sometimes a hefty amount.

They would retire with a sum of money, and spend just the interest and dividends – or the rent earned on a rental property – but didn't touch the initial sum, the capital. That was the inheritance, plus their home.

Most baby boomers, though, are thinking along different lines. Many will leave their home to their family, but plan to spend most of their savings during their retirement. And I expect the following generations will do the same.

There's logic to SKIing. Families tend to be much smaller than a generation ago, with many boomers having one, two or three children. If they inherit their parents' home, that's a fair chunk each. Also, houses these days are worth more, relative to other assets, than they used to be.

Should you SKI? A test: Unless your adult children have special needs or have had a particularly bad run of luck, hopefully they will be doing okay financially. Tell them you plan to spend your savings but retain your home. If they object, that might be a sign that they are selfish and perhaps don't deserve an inheritance anyway!

In the next part of this book, I'm assuming you plan to spend most of your retirement savings before you die.

A friend said to me recently, 'Fly first-class or your kids will.' It's food for thought.

Let's get on with goal setting

Look at your retirement savings goal as being made up of two components:

1. Money for regular spending
2. A lump sum

Your goal is the total of these two.

We'll look at regular spending first. And the good news is that you'll probably spend less in retirement than while you're working. You'll save by not having to pay:

- Work expenses: commuting, lunches, work clothes, dry cleaning, bought dinners and expensive pre-prepared food.

- Ideally, debt and mortgage repayments.
- Insurance. Around retirement time, or perhaps earlier, you may realise you no longer need life insurance. You can also stop insurance for loss of income. And other insurances, such as house and contents, are sometimes cheaper for older people. (But health insurance rises. More on that shortly.)
- The big one – saving. This may be taking a large chunk out of your income as you approach retirement. While some people keep saving until they die, retirement is really time to stop putting money away and start spending it.

I've been told off for adding another item to this list – the fact that you'll have time to do more for yourself, rather than paying others for things like cleaning, lawnmowing and gardening.

'That's all very well,' says a friend, 'but as you get older you become less able to do things like maintenance. I have to pay others to do lots of things I used to do around the house.'

But he has an unusually big property. Many retired people move to smaller sections or apartments partly to escape having to do maintenance. You'll have to judge how all this will apply in your circumstances.

Overall, though, retired people tend to spend less. And people in their eighties and older often say that their spending decreases further. That's simply because, in most cases, they travel less and go out less.

There are, of course, some things that cost more in retirement. The big one is health insurance. Premiums rise at an alarming rate as you get older, reflecting how much more medical care the elderly tend to need. But as you might remember, I recommend you don't drop health insurance despite the high premiums. For ideas on how you might keep premiums somewhat lower, refer back to 'Keeping insurance costs down' (page 50) in Step 3: 'Set up insurance – and a rainy day fund'.

Some simple calculations

After taking all of this into account, how much are you likely to want for regular spending in retirement?

Realistically, many of us think more in terms of 'How much will I be *able* to spend in retirement?' Here are some easy ways to get an idea of that. We'll start with a very simple calculation.

Rule of thumb 1: If you retire at 65 with X hundred thousand dollars, you can spend $X a week

For example, if your savings total $100,000, you can spend $100 a week above NZ Super. If you've saved $50,000, you can spend $50 a week, and if you've saved $500,000, you can spend $500 a week.

You'll be spending returns earned on your savings, but also gradually eating into the savings themselves – SKIing. But all the while the remaining savings are growing, with compounding returns.

Under this formula, your savings will probably last as long as you do. But if you live into your late eighties or older, you probably won't have a huge amount left over.

Want something a bit more sophisticated? Members of The Society of Actuaries – who are experts on money and statistics – have come up with some calculations about how far a retirement savings sum will go if you use up most or all of the money.

I've chosen two to look at here, which I've called Rules of Thumb 2 and 3. If you want to see two others, or read more about the assumptions made, go to www.tinyurl.com/RulesOfThumbNZ.

Rule of thumb 2: If you retire at 65, each year you can spend 6% of your savings at the start of retirement

If you save $100,000, you could spend $6,000 a year – or $115 a week, above NZ Super. With $50,000 it would be $3,000 a year or $58 a week, and with $500,000 it would be $30,000 a year or $577 a week.

If you invest your savings in a conservative fund – in or out of KiwiSaver – your money will almost certainly last until your mid eighties. And, depending on future returns, it may last until you're 90 or even 100.

You might have noticed that Rule 2 is a bit more generous than Rule 1.

An important point to note about both rules: If you retire *after* age 65, you will be able to spend more per week. That brings us to a third rule, which works regardless of your retirement age.

Rule of thumb 3: Divide your money by the years you want it to last

Say you retire at 70 and you want your money to last until you're 90 – after which, NZ Super should be enough.

In the first year, spend 1/20 of your savings, in the second year 1/19, and so on. In the second-to-last year you'll spend half of what's left of your savings, and in the final year you'll blow the lot and switch to NZ Super only – although of course you could choose instead to spread out your spending at that stage.

Unlike Rules 1 and 2, you won't know in advance exactly how much you can spend each week. That will vary a bit depending on the returns you earn on your savings in the meantime. But, also unlike the other two rules, you do know exactly how long your savings will last.

What about inflation?

How does inflation affect the rules? Good question.

Under Rules 1 and 2, you'll withdraw the same amount each year, but inflation will gradually decrease how much you can buy with that withdrawal.

But, as noted above, NZ Super – your other source of income – currently rises by more than inflation, and it seems unlikely it will rise by less than inflation in future. In any case, spending often decreases as people get older.

Rule 3 is much more inflation-proof. Because your savings will usually grow over the years, you will generally have more to spend each year.

I say 'usually' because if you have some of your savings in riskier investments – perhaps the savings you don't expect to spend for at least ten years – and the markets fall, you will have less to spend in the following year. More about how to invest your savings in retirement shortly.

Which rule of thumb should you use? It depends partly on the inflation issue, which favours Rule 3 if you want to spend more each year. But Rules 1 and 2 give you more certainty about your spending amount.

Given that you spend a bit less under Rule 1 than Rule 2, you're more likely to leave an inheritance (apart from your home), but you have a bit less fun along the way.

By now I hope you've got an idea of how much you would like to have for regular spending at the start of your retirement.

What about unexpected spending – such as a new roof, a better car, big medical bills, or happier things like a world trip? Many people like to start retirement with a good car and their home in good shape, but if you live into your nineties you might need another new car and new roof.

You'll want a lump sum to cover all these things, and only you can decide how much that should be. For some, $50,000 will do; for others, it might be half a million dollars.

Your retirement savings goal, then, is your total for regular spending plus your lump sum. Does it look out of reach? Read on. But first, a brightener.

The best is yet to come

The market research firm UMR has done surveys on what makes New Zealanders happy. Some of their findings bring good news for older Kiwis. They include:

- The happiest age group is those aged 75 and over, followed by those in their late sixties.
- The happiest occupation is 'retired', with around 37% of retirees scoring themselves 9 out of 10 or 10 out of 10 for happiness. (By the way, homemaker was the next happiest group, followed by professionals and managers.)
- When UMR looked at marital status, widows and widowers – whose spouses had died and they hadn't

remarried – were happier than married, de facto, divorced or never married people. About 29% of widowers and 35% of widows gave themselves high happiness scores.

There'll be more on this research in the last section of the book.

Making it easier

There are lots of ways you can make retirement easier financially. One obvious way is to retire later. As we've already discussed, younger readers are likely to find that NZ Super will start at an older age than 65. But many people are already retiring later than that age anyway.

This is no doubt partly because people in their mid sixties tend to be healthier than a generation ago, and they expect to live longer.

Workforce participation – part-time and full-time – for people aged 65 and over has soared in the past 30 years or so. According to Stats NZ, from 1990 to 2018, the percentage of people aged 65 to 69 in work more than quadrupled, from 10.2% to 44.5%; and the percentage of people aged 70 and over in work more than tripled, from 4.4% to 13.6%.

And the numbers, and percentages, of older workers are expected to keep rising. Working in your late sixties may become the norm.

Continuing to work has strong appeal for some people, the opposite for others. In a 2018 survey of people over 65, BNZ found two-thirds want to keep working because of the 'value and satisfaction it brings' or the ability to use their skills and talents. And more than half want to work for the social contact. However, close to a third said they need to work to get the money to pay their bills.

Whether you want to keep working or have to keep working as you get older, there are two pluses to doing so. For every year you keep working:

- You can save for one more year.
- You have one less year of retirement to fund with your savings.

Because of this double-barrelled effect, continuing to work past the usual retirement age can make a surprisingly big difference to how much you need to save for retirement.

How much? I worked through an example for a 50-year-old regular saver on an online retirement savings calculator. The relative spending numbers are what matter. I found:

- If that person retires at 65 they could spend $610 a week from their savings.
- If they retire at 67 it would be $730 a week.
- And if they work until 70 it would be $970 a week. That's more than one and a half times the amount at age 65.

'That's all very well,' you might be saying. 'But I'm not sure I'll be able to keep my job as I get older.'

There's no doubt that some employers discriminate on the basis of age. But you don't have to keep the same job, or even the same type of work.

What are you good at or love doing? Turn what was an interest into a part-time job. I've known people to make good money consulting, tutoring or teaching their hobby.

How about setting yourself up as a cake decorator or home handyman? One former chief executive of a large company thoroughly enjoys mowing lawns in his suburb, and chatting with the residents in the process.

Following are some other ways to make it easier to reach your retirement savings goal.

Move house

This idea can be a trap for old players. I've known people who have planned to free up several hundred thousand dollars by moving from their three- or four-bedroom suburban home to a much smaller place, only to find they didn't free up much at all.

The trouble is they wanted the new place to be low maintenance, perhaps close to bus routes, shops and health services, and with easy access. That's what lots of baby boomers want, so those places are not cheap.

Having said that, many people do, in fact, free up sums as large as half a million dollars or more by moving house – especially if they move out of a big city. You might protest that you want to stay close to family and friends. But with the willingness to jump in the car or take a train or bus – perhaps with SuperGold card in hand – you may be able to get around that.

If you plan to move towns, do take the time to get to know the destination town well, though. You don't want to get there and miss the restaurants, entertainment and bright lights. Perhaps rent out your big city home for six months or a year and rent in the small town on a trial basis.

Eat your house

It's common for retired people to be asset-rich and cash-poor. They own a home worth a small fortune, but are buying cheap peanut butter. If moving to a lower-priced home isn't a good option for you, there are other ways to make use of the value in your home.

Boarders or flatmates

Some people would rather struggle financially than take a stranger into their home. But I've known retired people to change their minds when they tried it, enjoying the company and the added security.

One friend who took in foreign students found it not only gave her extra income but also a much more diverse menu when the students taught her their ways of cooking.

Alternatives are to sublet a portion of your home – perhaps one wing or the downstairs – or to take in short-term 'company' through Airbnb, bookabach or similar schemes.

Note, though, that if you have others paying to stay in your home, you should tell your insurance company. While that might mean higher premiums, you want to be sure to have cover if, for example, the people staying with you get sticky fingers. You should also check your tax situation. See www.tinyurl.com/NZBoarderFlatmate.

True tale: Up in the air

'My sister has a prime waterfront spot,' says a reader of my *Weekend Herald* column, 'and she converted their downstairs into rental accommodation for Airbnb, and it has just taken off. They are earning more for their small two-room complex than my husband earns a week. People are in and out on a daily basis, and there are very few overheads, especially as she charges a cleaning fee. 'A great way to increase your retirement income,' she says. 'Who needs to save?'

My comments: With talk of bed taxes – and with some cities, including Auckland, charging higher rates for people who rent out part or all of their home on a short-term basis, and other cities considering similar action – this option probably won't remain as lucrative as it is now. Also, as more people get in on the act, competition will push down prices. You hear, too, of neighbours not welcoming the comings and goings, and that should be taken into account.

But still, this can be a good way to boost retirement income – if you don't mind sacrificing some privacy. And maybe that won't be an issue, depending on the layout of your home.

> **Moral:** There's gold in that thar home.

Subdivide

Many suburban properties are large enough to fit a second house on them – in some cases after the original house is moved a few metres. And some retired people would welcome the reduction in the size of their garden, and perhaps the security of having somebody else living nearby.

Don't dismiss the idea because you looked into it some years ago and found you weren't allowed to do it. In many bigger cities, zoning rules have changed and subdivision is now encouraged.

Rates rebate or postponement

Don't skip this, thinking you're not eligible. While rates rebates are for people on low incomes, including retirees, rates postponement varies. In some areas you have to be struggling, in others it's open to everyone.

Hardly anyone uses *rates postponement*, and that's a pity. It's a great way to free up perhaps several thousand dollars a year that could be spent on bills – or fun. I recommend you look into it in your retirement.

With rates postponement, you delay paying part or all of your rates until you sell the property or die. Basically, the council lends you the money in the meantime. And when the house is sold, the council gets its money back.

You pay relatively small upfront costs and possibly an ongoing fee, as well as fairly low interest. In Auckland, for example, the interest rate is the council's cost of borrowing, which will usually be well below mortgage rates.

The interest compounds over the years, but generally this is not a big deal. While your loan is growing, the value of your house will be growing faster in dollar terms. Sure, house prices might fall for a while, but over the long term they increase.

In any case, if you start worrying about the size of your loan you can always stop rates postponement from then on, which will slow the growth of the loan.

Different councils' policies vary. In most cases, you can pay back the rates plus interest, with no penalty, at any time if your circumstances change. You might, for example, inherit some money, and would like the interest clock to stop ticking.

For more info, go to www.tinyurl.com/NZPostponeRates. For Aucklanders, see www.tinyurl.com/AuckRatesPostponement.

A *rates rebate* is different. It's only for those on low incomes, and you don't have to repay the money. Rates rebates are run by local councils but paid for by central government. Your rates can be cut by up to $620 a year.

According to the Department of Internal Affairs website: 'How much you can claim depends on:

- how much your rates are — this includes local, regional and water rates
- your income, and
- whether you have any dependants, such as children, living with you.

'If your gross (before tax) income is $24,790 (about the same as NZ Super for a single living alone) or less you can often claim the full amount. If your income is higher you may still be able to get all or part of the rebate depending on:

- how much your rates are, and
- how many children or other dependants are in your household.'

In 2018 the rules were changed so that retirement village residents who don't own their unit, but pay fees to live there, can also claim a rates rebate.

For more info, see www.tinyurl.com/nzRatesRebate. For Aucklanders, there's more info at www.tinyurl.com/AuckRatesRebate.

Reverse mortgage

This is rates postponement on steroids. You borrow money, often from a bank, in an arrangement similar to an ordinary mortgage, but you generally make no repayments until you sell the property or die.

The important differences from rates postponement are:

- The interest rate will almost always be considerably higher.
- You can borrow much more than the amount of your rates.

For these two reasons, the loan can grow big – frighteningly big for some people. But keep reading. In the right circumstances, reverse mortgages can be a great idea. I'm thinking of getting one myself in my very old age. Basically, I plan to spend my savings until I'm 90, and then live on NZ Super and a reverse mortgage – for the next 20 years or so!

Over the years, several different banks have offered reverse mortgages for a time, and then stopped. I don't think there's been a huge uptake. But also some bankers have said the fact that they charge fairly high interest can lead to negative feelings about the bank.

The interest rate – perhaps a couple of percentage points above ordinary mortgages – is probably justified though. For one thing, these mortgages are somewhat riskier for banks because they grow bigger over time, and the banks don't know when they'll be repaid. For another, the banks say they need to spend a lot of time explaining the product to people. One bank used to hold three meetings with customers before signing them up, in an effort to make sure they understood what they were doing.

I'm sure all providers would also insist you discussed a reverse mortgage with a lawyer.

Usually, you can borrow only quite a small portion of your equity (the value of the property minus any mortgage you have). The amount you can borrow increases as you get older – because there's less time for the loan to grow.

The lender will want to protect their equity. That means you've got to keep the house fully insured, pay your rates, and maintain the property. But you would probably do that anyway.

Because a reverse mortgage can grow big over the years, I don't recommend getting one in your sixties or early seventies – unless you're in poor health. But consider it for later in retirement.

You might find there are only one or two providers offering them. Talk to your own bank, too. Even though most banks don't announce it, some will set one up for a customer.

If you have adult children, it's a good idea to discuss what's happening with them. If they are expecting to inherit your home, they otherwise might get a rude shock when they find a bank owns half or more of it. But don't skip a reverse mortgage just because of the kids. Remember, we're SKIing!

Questions to ask about reverse mortgages:

- Will you have the right to live in the property for life, no matter how long you live?
- What happens if you move to another property, or go into care for what is intended to be a temporary period but it drags on?
- Is there a guarantee you won't owe more than the proceeds from selling your property? You will usually get this important guarantee, but you should check.
- How will the loan affect your estate when you die?
- Can you set aside part of your equity in the property (house value minus mortgage), so that there's

something left for the kids or nieces and nephews to inherit? This will mean you can borrow less.

If you decide to get a reverse mortgage, try to get a flexible one, and borrow only as much as you want or need at the time, adding more later. Don't get extra money that will sit in a bank account earning much less interest than you are paying on the loan. That's dumb! If you keep the loan amount low for as long as possible, there's less interest to compound.

I suggest you also do a Google search on reverse mortgages. You will probably come up with the latest Consumer NZ article on the topic. Read it. As I've said before, if you're not a member of Consumer NZ and so can't get access to the article, join!

Examples of a reverse mortgage

Heartland Bank, which offers reverse mortgages, has some handy calculators at www.seniorsfinance.co.nz.

They show, for example, that if you're 65 and your house is worth $600,000, you can borrow up to $120,000. If you're 75 you can borrow $180,000, and if you're 85 it's $240,000.

Double those amounts if your house is worth twice as much. For example, at 65 with a house worth $1.2 million, you can borrow $240,000. At 75 it's $360,000 and at 85 it's $480,000.

Let's look further at the situation if you're 75, and your house is worth $600,000. You decide to borrow $50,000, and the bank charges you 7.82% (compared with its floating rate at the time of writing of 5.85%).

The bank assumes house values rise by a fairly conservative 3% a year.

- By 80, the loan will total $74,000 and your house value will be $696,000.
- By 85, the loan will total $109,000 and your house value will be $806,000.
- By 90, the loan will total $161,000 and your house value will be $935,000.
- By 95, the loan will total $238,000 and your house value will be $1,084,000.

Your loan more than triples while the house value less than doubles – because the loan is growing at a faster pace. But the gap between the two numbers keeps increasing. You're fine. If you die or move out at 95, you or your heirs will get $1,084,000 minus $238,000, which is $846,000.

Maths alert! However, if you borrowed the maximum you're allowed at 75 – $180,000 – the loan would grow to $856,000 by the time you were 95. Meanwhile, your house would be worth the same $1,084,000 as above.

With this higher loan amount, the gap between the two numbers decreases over time. If you lived well past 100, the gap would disappear. But there's no need to panic: as of October 2018 the Heartland Bank offers a No Negative Equity Guarantee, which means, it says, 'that you will not have to pay us back more than the net sale proceeds of the property, even if this amount is less than the outstanding loan balance'.

Main point: If you borrow a larger amount, the gap between the loan and your house value may decrease.

Don't forget, though, that the bank is assuming house prices will rise by 3% a year. They may well rise faster.

Play around with the calculator, to get a feel for how the numbers might work for you.

Sell your house and become a tenant in another house

Most homeowners would dismiss this idea outright. They have owned their own home, with the freedom to do what they want and the knowledge that no landlord can kick them out. Who would want to lose that?

But some might be happy to trade those advantages for not having to worry about maintenance and so on – being able to just call the landlord when things go wrong.

And financially they could be onto a big winner. The proceeds from selling some houses these days could buy you many years of rent plus some wonderful trips and a luxurious lifestyle.

It's not a silly idea, especially if you could get a long-term lease. There are probably plenty of landlords who would love to have a retired person as a long-term tenant.

Sell assets

Are you using the bach or the second car or the boat less and less as you get older? Consider turning them into cash. And then there's the smaller stuff. Selling is so much easier these days, using the internet. If you're not familiar with how Trade Me works, learn. It's fun. And you'll be surprised at how much some of the junk sitting around your place will sell for.

Take the time to clean up the items and take appealing photos of them. Other photos on Trade Me might give you some ideas about how to 'pose' your items.

Consider, too, selling some of your valuables. I'm not suggesting you part with the paintings or ornaments or jewellery you love. But we all have some items we've fallen out of love with, or maybe never really liked, if we're honest. Sell a few pieces and fund a holiday. Why not?

A bonus of selling things is that you free up space and simplify your life. And let's be honest here – whoever ends up going through your stuff after you've passed on to the Place Where Money Doesn't Matter will be very glad they have less to go through.

A word of warning: you don't want to sell something only to find that one of your heirs particularly loved it. So perhaps talk to them first. It's a good idea to have that conversation anyway. You can then be sure you leave the right things to the right people.

What if I live to be very old?

As we've already discussed, old old people don't tend to spend much, and many say they find NZ Super is plenty. And rates postponement or a reverse mortgage can work well at this stage, with not many years of compounding interest.

But if you're still worried, here's a trick. Leave some money in your will for charity. If you live past 90, you become the charity! At that stage, change the will and spend the money.

Investing during retirement

One – very important – way to make your savings go further is to take more risk in the run-up and during retirement. As you must know by now, this will give you higher returns, on average over time. The tricky part is that in retirement you are planning to spend your savings, no longer locking the money away.

However, unless you retire at an unusually old age, or you're in poor health, you will probably start retirement expecting to live for 15, 20 or 30 more years. So you don't need to do what many people do at retirement – putting all their savings in conservative investments like bank term deposits.

Definitely do that with the money you plan to spend in the next three years or so. But if you're wise you'll put:

- the three-to-ten-year money in bonds or a balanced fund – in or out of KiwiSaver;
- the money for ten years plus in a KiwiSaver or non-KiwiSaver share fund or similar.

Every year, move some money from the share fund to the balanced fund or bonds, and some from there to term deposits, so you keep to the three-year and ten-year cut-offs.

This will mean your savings are more volatile. But by now I hope you're feeling braver about that.

In our Rule of Thumb 2 earlier in this chapter, the Society of Actuaries assumed your savings earned 3.5% a year on average, after tax, throughout retirement. But if you use the plan above, you'll probably earn a higher average return. That means you can spend a bit more or leave more to your heirs.

Apart from keeping some retirement savings in riskier investments, follow all the same rules concerning investing that we've already talked about – diversify, largely ignore past performance, don't try to time markets, and don't trade frequently. Just because you've retired doesn't mean any of that changes.

KiwiSaver in retirement

KiwiSaver can have a big role in your retirement. Once you get to 65, you can withdraw your KiwiSaver money whenever you want to – unless you've been in the scheme for less than five years, in which case you must wait until the five years are up. (If proposed changes go ahead, the five-year lock-in will no longer apply to people who join after 1 July 2019, but will continue to apply to people who joined before that date.)

When you get access to the money, your tax credits stop. If you're still working, your employer is allowed to also stop contributions, although many don't. If your employer keeps contributing, that's an extra reason to stay in the scheme.

But in any case, stay in. Even if you want to empty your account to pay off a mortgage, for example, keep at least a few dollars there. Once you've closed the account, if you're 65 or over you can't open it again. (Under the proposed changes, though, anyone will be able to join KiwiSaver at any age.) And KiwiSaver can work well in retirement for medium- and long-term money.

Just one note of caution. People often comment that their KiwiSaver account is bringing in higher returns than a bank term deposit, so they use it for their short-term savings in retirement.

That's a worry. Unless you're in a very low-risk defensive fund – in which case your returns may not be higher than bank term deposits anyway – your KiwiSaver account will have some volatility. That's not a good idea for money you're about to spend.

Laddering

This is a good way to set up your term deposits or bonds. You can do this at any time in your life, but it tends to be more useful in retirement because you're spending rather than saving, so you're likely to have more money in term deposits and bonds then.

Let's say you want to hold your money in two-year term deposits because, in most circumstances, you'll get higher interest than if you went for a shorter term.

Divide your money into, say, four lots. So if you've got $100,000 to invest, put:

- $25,000 in a six-month deposit;
- $25,000 in a one-year deposit;
- $25,000 in an 18-month deposit;
- $25,000 in a two-year deposit.

Then, as each term deposit matures, reinvest it for two years. Figure 15 shows how this is done.

Figure 15: Laddering $100,000
X is the year the deposit matures; you then reinvest it for 2 years

	Jan. '19	July '19	Jan. '20	July '20	Jan. '21	July '21	Jan. '22	July '22	Jan. '23	July '23	Jan. '24
$25,000		X				X				X	
$25,000			X				X				X
$25,000				X				X			
$25,000					X				X		

The advantages of laddering are:

- You have some money maturing every six months, in case you need it.
- After a while, all your money is in two-year deposits, earning usually higher interest.
- You won't miss out entirely if interest rates rise. If they go up after you've set up your laddering, at least some of your money will mature soon to catch that rise. If rates fall, of course, the opposite happens. Some of your money will be reinvested at lower rates. But you'll still have some money in at the old rates!

Rental property in retirement

As I explained in Step 5: 'Boost your saving painlessly', I have reservations about investing in rental property. It's riskier than many people realise. And in retirement I think it can be even less suitable, because you can't spend your capital – the money you bought the house with.

Sure, you receive rent. And by retirement you might have paid off the mortgage and so you keep a fair bit of the rent – after tax, rates, insurance and maintenance. But you've still got lots of money tied up in the house – money that you could be spending on fun.

However, I was recently put in my place by a man who told me he loves being a landlord in his retirement. He now has lots of time to work on his properties, adding value for himself, his tenants and his heirs. If that's you, and you have plenty of income from rental properties or other sources, go for it! If your rental properties are mortgage-free, the investment is much lower risk.

True tale: Choose an adviser with care

A letter that I received nearly ten years ago for my *Weekend Herald* Q&A column shocked me. It was from a couple who were deeply worried about their retirement savings.

They had sold the family bach for $2 million, and gone to a financial adviser to find out where to invest the money. He had put them into two similar complex fixed-term investments, and since then the couple had watched in horror as their value fell to $1.6 million.

What's more, they discovered that their initial expectation – that they would get their money back at the end – was not guaranteed.

It was a classic case of terrible diversification – just two investments, and both of the same type. Also, the adviser had failed to inform them of key characteristics of the investments.

As it turned out, many advisers were receiving generous commissions if they put clients into those investments. It doesn't take a genius to guess that might have had something to do with the man's advice.

Sadly for the couple, their only course of action was to hire a lawyer to try to get compensation.

The law has changed since then, thank goodness, and every provider of financial services must belong to a dispute resolution scheme. (For more information on dispute resolution schemes, see 'If you have a problem' (page 142) in Step 5: 'Boost your saving painlessly'.)

Also, financial advisers are now more regulated, and are supposed to put clients' interests before their own. (I wouldn't count on that, though. For tips on how to pick an adviser who is much more likely to do well for you, see

'One more thing: Do you need personal financial advice?'
towards the end of this book.)

> **Moral:** Not all advice is good. Also, if you
> understand financial basics – like the importance
> of diversification – it's much less likely you will end
> up in a situation like this. You've been reading this
> book, so you can already tick that box!

Step 7 check

Have you:

- ❏ Worked through the life expectancy calculator?
- ❏ Considered our rules of thumb on retirement spending?
- ❏ Set an approximate savings goal?
- ❏ Thought about how you will make it easier to fund your retirement?
- ❏ Worked out how you will invest in retirement?

Reward

Chocolates, cheese or flowers; or a 'me day' with a walk, book, time with family, being creative; or donating to a charity, or anything else that makes you smile.

What's next? Let's weigh up the pros and cons – and hows – of home ownership.

Step

?

(WHEN IT'S THE RIGHT TIME – IF EVER)

BUY A HOME, OR SELL ONE

In which we ...

- Realise there's a lot to be said for never owning a home
- Can't go past KiwiSaver if you do plan on buying
- Consider becoming a renter-landlord, or a floating homeowner
- List essentials for home buyers

- Plan an auction strategy
- Consider all the mortgage bells and whistles
- Look into why and how to pay off a mortgage faster
- Smarten up a house for sale
- Learn how to inspire an agent to get you more when you sell a house

There's no right stage of life to buy a home. Some frighteningly good planners and savers are in their first home in their early twenties. For others it might be in their retirement – or never. That's why I haven't numbered this step. Slot it in where it suits you.

That doesn't mean it's not important, though. Buying a home, or making a decision not to buy one and planning accordingly, is a key part of financial security. Let's look first at deciding not to buy.

Not planning on home ownership

You don't have to ever own a home to be financially well set up. This goes against the grain for many New Zealanders. We've been raised to dream of having a place of our own. But house prices – at least in 2018 – are out of whack with incomes, and out of reach for many would-be first home buyers.

It won't always be that way. How do I know? Just by looking at history.

From the 1950s to the late 1980s, the average New Zealand house price was 2 to 3 times the average household annual income. Then house prices gradually rose, to 6.5 times income in 2008. They then dropped, but have since risen to about that level again. In Auckland, meantime, house prices in 2018 were more than 9 times annual household income.

That is way out of line. Generally, around the world, houses cost about three times household income – as they did here for 30-odd years just a few decades ago.

People have a tendency to think that whatever has been going on in the share or property markets for a while will continue, but it never does. House prices, as a multiple of average incomes, will fall again. It's just that we don't know when.

In the meantime, rather than complaining, if you feel shut out of the housing market think in terms of getting on with your life as a renter – and possibly staying that way for the rest of your life. You can always change your mind later.

Many people in Europe rent for life. In Germany, the home ownership rate is just over 50%, and in Switzerland it's lower still. And they are not poor countries – far from it. These Europeans are happy to remain as tenants, usually with very long-term leases. It's not uncommon to live in the same rented property all your adult life. The people treat their rented accommodation as their homes in a way that only homeowners usually do in New Zealand.

The circumstances in those countries are quite different from here. For one thing, the law tends to favour tenants more. Still, the tide might be turning in New Zealand. In a recent Consumer NZ survey of people who were renting accommodation, 64% said they rented because they can't afford to buy. But another 26% said 'It suits my lifestyle right now' and 5% said 'I like the flexibility of renting'.

It would be great if some landlords offered tenants longer-term leases – perhaps after a trial tenancy of, say, a year. That could suit both sides.

Weighing up the finances

Despite what your parents and others might say, renting for life doesn't have to be a bad decision financially.

> **Key message:** You can do fine as long as you reach retirement with lots of extra savings – preferably several hundred thousand dollars – to cover the costs of your accommodation for the rest of your life.

That might sound difficult – saving a whole lot more than people who own a home – but it doesn't have to be.

Generally, it costs considerably more throughout life to own a home than to rent accommodation of a similar standard. Not only do you have to pay mortgage interest, but also rates, house insurance and maintenance. If you save the difference, and invest it wisely over the years, you might even end up better off than your homeowner friend on about the same income as you.

How do you know how much to save? Ask how much your friend spends on having her or his own home.

I've seen various calculations of who becomes better off – the homeowner or renter. The answer always depends on the assumptions you make. We could make one set of reasonable assumptions about house prices, mortgage interest, insurance, rates, maintenance, rent and returns on savings, and the homeowner would win. But with another set, the renter would win.

One thing is certain: if you're a renter you won't win unless you are:

- Disciplined about saving. It's not clever to live the high life because your accommodation costs are cheaper. The best way to keep the savings rolling in is to set up an automatic transfer every payday.
- Willing to make higher-risk investments with your savings, so they get higher returns on average. A good choice would be a KiwiSaver or non-KiwiSaver growth or aggressive fund, which holds mostly shares. As you know by now, with these investments your balance will sometimes fall, but you need to stick with it through thick and thin.

You can probably transfer your savings directly from your bank account into a growth fund or, if the provider doesn't take small regular savings, into a savings account, which you empty into the growth fund every now and then.

One clear financial advantage for the renter over the homeowner is that your savings can be more diversified. If you're in a growth fund, you will be in a wide range of shares and probably also some bonds and other assets.

Weighing up other issues

An obvious negative of renting is that your landlord can kick you out. That would be especially bad if you have children – although longer-term leases could help reduce that risk.

Also, in most cases you don't get to choose the carpets, paint colours, curtains and so on – although, again, you might with a longer lease.

There may be similar issues with the garden. If you're a keen gardener, you'll want some kind of guarantee that you won't be asked to move out just when the vegies are coming into their own, or the hedge is getting bushier. And if you enjoy DIY or renovation projects, you can't build up value in the property by adding a deck.

Also, over the longer term, you won't have a property for your children to inherit. And there's less security for your retirement in a rented property, although you could perhaps use your savings to buy a small home at that stage.

But there are some big advantages to renting:

- You don't have to worry about maintenance and other responsibilities that can sometimes weigh heavily, both financially and psychologically, on a homeowner. As I once heard someone say, 'Did you have a good weekend, or do you own your own home?' If you're renting and the roof starts to leak, you just call the landlord.
- It's often easier for a renter to live close to downtown, which can be a big plus in these times of terrible rush-hour traffic.
- You can move house much more easily and cheaply than a homeowner.
- If you want to set up your own business, you could use some of your savings to do that, whereas a homeowner may have to raise a loan by adding to their mortgage.

For some people, none of this is as important as the pride of home ownership and the fact that you have more control over your living environment. But for others, the freedom that comes with renting is a big attraction.

True tale: Who needs home ownership?

A friend of mine, who helps businesses find money to expand, tells of a couple who suddenly received a windfall of about $750,000 when a company was sold.

'They are from San Francisco, had migrated to New Zealand and were in their mid forties at the time, with two children in their late teens or early twenties,' says my friend. 'They had no debt and wanted to discuss investment options.

'I asked if they owned a house. They said, "No," and then explained that they are mystified by New Zealanders' obsession with home ownership. They were very happy to be renters and had absolutely no interest in owning a home. They said in San Francisco's Bay Area very few people their age aspire to own a home.

'This doesn't appear to be related to affordability. Rather, it is a preference to invest in other assets, once they are in a position to invest.

'These are normal, sensible people, moderately well off but certainly not rich. Other than their accents, they are just like any other Kiwi of their age. I understand that this attitude is the norm in Europe, too, especially Germany.'

My friend continues, 'With the obsession New Zealanders have with home ownership, and the "woe-is-me" hand-wringers who are distraught about declining levels of home ownership, I often wonder if it really is that sensible as a cornerstone of one's investments.

'The widespread attitude seems to be that the first investment Kiwis make is a home. And only after you get rid of the mortgage do you start thinking about other investments. If you don't own a home you are somehow a failure. This seems to me to be totally wrong-headed as the basis of sensible personal investment.'

> **Moral:** Buying a home is not the only way to financial security.

Saving to buy a first home

Still, most New Zealanders want to own their own home. And in most circumstances, the best way to save for a home is in KiwiSaver. (An exception to this will be described in 'Thinking creatively', below.)

As you've already read ('Help to buy a home' (page 68) in Step 4: 'Join the best KiwiSaver fund for you'), everyone can withdraw their KiwiSaver money, except $1,000, to buy a first home. And people on lower incomes may also qualify for extra money from the government. What's more, some people with modest assets who previously owned a home, but don't now, may also be able to get a grant.

Even if you're not eligible for a grant, you'll save much more in KiwiSaver than elsewhere. Your savings will be boosted by the tax credit and, in many cases, by employer contributions.

The only possible negative is that you have to be in KiwiSaver for at least three years before you can make the withdrawal, and you have to contribute at a certain level to get the grant.

Some people worry that the rules could be changed, making them unable to withdraw their KiwiSaver money for a home purchase, but I can't imagine that happening. There would be such an outcry that I reckon no government would dare to do it.

Having said that, you might want to put your *extra* savings – over and above 3% of your pay if you are an employee, or $1,043 a year if you're not – into a similar non-KiwiSaver fund, perhaps run by the same provider. That gives you more flexibility. Check, though, that the fees are not much higher than in KiwiSaver.

If you're saving for a first home, how risky should your KiwiSaver or other fund be? It's the same rule as before. If you plan to buy the house within two or three years, you're best off in a low-risk fund. If it's three to ten years away, a balanced fund is good. If it's more than ten years before you expect to buy, and you can tolerate the ups and downs, choose a growth or even an aggressive fund.

The rules for withdrawing your KiwiSaver money to buy a first home are fairly straightforward. But still, check with your provider well in advance of buying to make sure you cross all the 'T's and dot the 'I's. And if you're hoping to get a grant, it's important that you read the rules. Some people have got tripped up if they were, for example, buying land first and planning to build on it later.

Also, the government has adjusted the income and house price caps several times, and that's likely to continue. And a few other rules have also been changed. So keep an eye on www.tinyurl.com/NZFirstHomeHelp.

Note that you can be pre-approved for a grant before you find a home. The pre-approval lasts 180 days. If you haven't bought within that time, you need to apply again.

Be in for a chance with KiwiBuild

In mid-2018 the government started to take registrations for its KiwiBuild program, under which it plans to 'deliver 100,000 affordable, quality homes over the next decade'.

This is entirely separate from KiwiSaver help for first home buyers. Eligible people go into a ballot for the chance to buy a newly built home.

If you're in the market to buy a home, you can read more about KiwiBuild and perhaps register your interest at www. kiwibuild.govt.nz.

You have to be a first home buyer or someone who qualifies as a previous homeowner under the asset test for the KiwiSaver HomeStart grant (refer back to page 70, 'Previous homeowners', in Step 4: 'Join the best KiwiSaver fund for you').

But the rules are different from the KiwiSaver HomeStart rules. You must intend to live in the home for at least three years. And single purchasers must have an income below $120,000. For couples, the income cap is $180,000.

The price caps for the houses in Auckland and Queenstown are: $500,000 for a one-bedroom house, $600,000 for two bedrooms, and $650,000 for three or more bedrooms. In other areas, there is an overall price cap of $500,000.

Note that income and price caps may change. Check the website.

Thinking creatively

If you can't afford to buy near where you work and want to live, one way to get into the property market is to become a 'renter-landlord'.

In a 2018 survey, BNZ asked 'aspiring first home buyers' what they were prepared to do to get on the property ladder. About 44% – mainly in Auckland or Wellington – said they would buy a property and rent it out, either in a cheaper part of their city or somewhere else in New Zealand.

The basic idea is presumably that you're 'in the market' if property prices keep rising fast, making it easier to buy your own home later. It's not a bad idea, but you need to go in with your eyes open.

For one thing, you'll probably kiss goodbye to KiwiSaver first home help. You can't buy a rental property using your KiwiSaver money or a HomeStart grant. Those are available only if you live in the house for at least six months after buying it. And if you want to buy your own home later, you won't be eligible for the withdrawal or grant because you already own a property, says a Housing NZ spokesperson.

'Clearly, if they sold the rental, then they could apply as a previous homeowner, once they no longer owned any interest in (real) estate. However, it would mean that they have to meet the realisable assets test, which would not be required if they were first home buyers,' he adds.

If you go back to the section 'Previous homeowners' (page 70) in Step 4: 'Join the best KiwiSaver fund for you', you'll see that your 'realisable assets' have to total less than 20% of the house price cap for existing properties in the area where you plan to buy. Realisable assets would include the proceeds you've made from selling the rental, plus all the other things listed in that section. So chances are your assets would be too high – especially if you've made gains on the rental property.

There's one way around this. If you're thinking of buying a rental in a cheaper part of town – as opposed to elsewhere in New Zealand – you could buy the property as your own home and live in it for at least six months, and then move elsewhere while keeping it as a rental. Or who knows? Maybe you'll discover you like living there!

There are also other concerns about becoming a renter-landlord:

- These days, in most cases you need a higher deposit – 35% at the time of writing – to buy a rental property compared with 20% for your own home. Still, 35% of $300,000 in a cheaper area is $105,000. That's way less than 20% of $1 million ($200,000) in a posher suburb.
- If you sell the property within five years, you will probably be taxed on your gains under the so-called 'bright line' rules introduced in 2018.
- Owning a rental property is not easy. Read the section titled 'Rental property' on page 132.
- Property prices in many parts of the country seem to be slowing or even falling, and it wouldn't be surprising if there are more widespread falls in the next few years. Also, price rises tend to vary hugely around the country, and even from suburb to suburb. Be prepared to possibly have to sell at a loss.

Sorry to be a wet blanket. The idea might still work well for you.

Other results of the BNZ survey of aspiring first home buyers:

- 30% of the people would buy a shared property with their family.
- 21% would go 'tiny' and buy an apartment or unit under 80 square metres to live in, and another 12% would buy a tiny apartment or unit in another town to rent it out.
- 14% would buy a shared property with friends.
- 19% would buy land outside of the city they live in.

All these ideas have merit. Tiny properties are a bit of a trend, which goes hand in hand with the idea that we all have too much stuff. But you might want to try out the idea first by living in a caravan for more than a few weeks!

Getting help from family members – often parents or even grandparents – to buy a first home is becoming increasingly common. If you share a purchase with family or friends, I recommend you work out in advance what you will do if someone is unable to make agreed payments for a period, or if a relationship break-up changes how things work, or if somebody becomes disabled or dies. Be pessimistic. It's much better to work these things out in advance than when the crisis happens.

Then put all the details into a formal agreement drawn up by a lawyer. That sounds heavy and unnecessary, but I've seen families and great friendships break up for the want of such an agreement.

A floating home

In early 2016, I ran a series of readers' letters in my *Weekend Herald* column about living in a boat on a marina.

One correspondent reported that the upfront cost can be as little as $70,000 to $80,000 for a boat, marina licence and secure parking. Another said a 40-foot boat costs about $50,000 to $80,000, and a marina berth $7,000 to $9,000 a year. The bigger the boat, the more the berth costs. There can also be a 'live aboard fee'.

One reader warned that boats shouldn't be seen as investments. You're unlikely to get back your purchase price plus what you've spent on maintenance – which costs about 10% of the boat's price each year, and more if you're not handy.

She added that not everyone wants to live in such close quarters with their partner or family, as there's very little privacy. And in many cases you have to use public facilities for washing and showering. Still, she said, it's wonderful to be able to head off in your home for weekends and holidays away. There's some appeal in that!

Making the purchase of a first or subsequent home

Whether you're buying your first home or your 17th home, you may be tempted to try to time the market – waiting for prices to fall if they have been rising. Don't. You might end up putting your life on hold for years, while prices keep climbing. As someone once said, 'The best time to buy a home is always five years ago.'

Sure, you'll be unhappy if you buy and then prices fall soon after, but it's best to take a philosophical attitude to that. Over the years, you're quite likely to buy and sell several homes. You will probably have good luck with your timing sometimes and bad luck sometimes. That's life!

It's important to note, when you're looking for a home to buy, that real estate agents are paid by sellers and are there to represent them – not you. Of course they'll be friendly to you. They can't get a deal through without a keen buyer. But they're not acting in your interests.

Remember back in Step 5: 'Boost your saving painlessly' we were talking about scams and I said don't ever give in to pressure from salespeople? The same applies to buying property. There's usually no scamming going on, but agents can be adept at making you think someone else is about to buy the property and you'd better get your offer in fast.

Sometimes it's true of course. But if another person does make an offer, the agent should at least get back to you to see if you want to offer more.

> **Key message:** Buying a house is a big decision. Do not let anyone pressure you into making that decision quickly.

If you're seriously thinking of buying a property:

- Get hold of a LIM – or land information memorandum – on the property. This is issued by the local council, and gives you info on things like: rates; potential erosion, slippage or flooding; drains on the land; possible health hazards; and resource planning consents. LIMs usually cost around $250 to $400, so ask the agent listing the property if you can get a copy of the most recent LIM from them. If not, it's worth getting your own.
- Go to the property at different times of the day, and perhaps during the week and on the weekend, to check how much sun it gets, whether there's a noise problem, and whether there's always plenty of parking for you and your visitors.
- Check out the neighbourhood. How close are schools, public transport and shops, and how good do they look? You might not need a school or a bus, but it will affect the value of your property when you come to sell later. You can learn quite a lot just by driving by and walking around, or perhaps knocking on a neighbour's door.
- Go to www.qv.co.nz to get the rating valuation of the property, and the others near it. That's free, but you

can also pay to get more info on the property. It's worth spending a bit of time on this website. Another website to explore is www.homes.co.nz.

- Hire a registered builder or other qualified house inspector to check out the property. If at all possible, go with him or her on the inspection. They will give you a written report later, with photos, but you learn more if you're on the spot. The inspector might, for example, point out a defect or dampness problem, and you can discuss how it might be fixed and what it might cost. If you can, get into the attic and under the house with the inspector to check things like insulation and foundations. It's surprising what you'll learn.

A building inspection will cost you several hundred dollars. Before spending the money, consider asking the seller's agent if you can make an offer on the property conditional upon getting a satisfactory inspection. If they baulk, you've got to wonder why.

> **Key message:** If after doing all this you can't negotiate a reasonable price for the property, you must be prepared to walk away.

It may be hard. By now you've probably been thinking about where your furniture would go, what colour you would paint the dining room, and how you would change the garden. You might also think this is the only place for you. But it's not. Believe me, because I've been there more than once. You will find another even better place.

Buying at an auction

Auctions have been more common around Auckland than elsewhere in New Zealand, but still you might find yourself bidding in an auction anywhere around the country.

If you plan to do this, it's important to go to some other auctions first and watch how they work. It's quite fun, actually, and there can be sometimes be a bit of drama.

When it comes to the auction you're interested in, rule number one is that you set a maximum bid before the auction, and *do not* bid past it. If you pay too much for a property, it can really knock you back financially. You must go to every auction being prepared to lose.

A lot is written about bidding techniques. Who knows how good the advice is? But one trick I've found that has worked several times is to not bid at all until it seems the last bid has been made. The auctioneer is, perhaps, raising his or her gavel, ready to call, 'Sold.' Then you make your bid. What's more, you jump the price. If the last few bids have been $1,000 apart, you jump by $3,000. For example, the bids go $672,000, $673,000, $674,000, and then you say $677,000.

The last bidder will not be happy, but that's the game. In their despondency, they will quite often stop bidding, and the place is yours.

Normally you can't put conditions on buying at auction. However, you can always approach the seller's agent beforehand and explain that you will bid only if there's a prior written agreement that if you win you will buy under certain conditions. I did that once when I needed a longer settlement date, and it worked fine.

If you can't get an agreement like that, and you're not prepared to bid without it, all is not lost. Quite often, especially in quieter markets, the property will be passed in because the bidding doesn't reach the seller's minimum price, known as the reserve. The agent – who knows you by then because you've tried to get the agreement – should at that stage come back to you. At that point you can make a conditional offer.

True tale: Sell before you buy

Remember back a few steps when I wrote about losing 30% on a house? That was partly because the housing market had plunged, but also because my husband and I had to sell in a hurry. We had already bought another house, and were facing huge double mortgage payments.

The situation arose – as these things often do – because we fell in love with a house with a sea view that was just down the road from close friends. It was being sold by auction, so we couldn't make an offer conditional upon selling our old place for at least a certain price. We took the risk and bought anyway – paying not much more than what we thought our old place was worth. After all, we figured, we were buying and selling in the same market.

In the weeks that followed, we did all we could to sell our old house at a reasonable price. But there's only so much you can do while waiting for buyers to come. In the end we took the house to auction. Lots of people – including nosy neighbours – turned up, the house looked attractive in the sunshine, and the bidding seemed to start well.

But then the auctioneer took us aside. In those days, an auctioneer could pretend to be taking bids if there were no real ones, and that's exactly what he was doing. Nobody had made a single bid. I'll never forget hearing that. A few days later we sold the house for a song – just to end the nightmare.

Clearly, house prices had dropped much more in our old suburb than in the new one. But it wasn't just that. We were desperate sellers because we had already bought our next house.

I know, I know … you want to buy before you sell because you're fussy. You may not want to move at all unless it's to a place you really like. And if you see the place of your dreams, you'll want to grab it, and worry about selling the old place later. But that's a risky strategy, as I learnt.

It's far better to have sold first, for these reasons:

- You know exactly how much money you have. Also, you're a 'cash buyer', which puts you in a stronger position to negotiate.
- The ball is in your court. If you've already signed a deal to sell your old place, you can spend every spare minute looking at houses, which is so much better than sitting around hoping somebody will buy your old property.
- It's better to end up with no house for a while – staying with friends or family or doing a deal with a local motel or hotel or Airbnb – than having to pay two mortgages or expensive bridging finance.

Tip: If you sell first, ask your buyers if they would like a long settlement period. That gives you more time to find a new place, and often it suits the other side, too. Don't just accept what the agent tells you is the standard period.

> **Moral:** Back in Step 6: 'Stay cool' I talked about never getting yourself in a position where you're forced to sell. That applies to homes as much as to investments. ·

The mortgage maze

A mortgage, a lawyer friend tells me, is strictly speaking not a loan, but a document that outlines how the loan is secured by a property. But to most of the world, a mortgage is the loan itself. And if you don't pay it back, the lender can sell the property to get their money back.

We've already talked about mortgages several times in this book:

- In Step 2: 'Kill off high-interest debt' we looked at reducing your mortgage versus investing.
- In Step 4: 'Join the best KiwiSaver fund for you' we looked more specifically at that question versus investing in KiwiSaver.
- In Step 5: 'Boost your saving painlessly' we looked at taking out a mortgage to buy a rental property, and how the lucky geared investor did very well but the unlucky one ended up with no property and a debt to the bank.

Those lucky and unlucky examples also apply to someone borrowing to buy their own home. And, occasionally, there's a similar sad ending if the homeowner is forced to sell. Usually, though, people don't give up their home without a fight. And let's face it – few of us could buy our first home without getting a mortgage.

In this section, we'll look in more depth at what for most people is by far the biggest debt they take on in their lives. And it's not just the debt, but the interest on it. It's not uncommon for you to end up paying back twice what you borrowed or more over the course of a mortgage.

If you just blunder into the mortgage maze, you can wind up much worse off than you need to be. It's well worth knowing your way around.

Let's start with a warning: Just because a bank will give you a mortgage of a certain size doesn't mean you will find it easy to repay it. Sometimes the banks have plenty of money sloshing around and are too keen to lend. Don't rely on the lender – work out for yourself whether you can manage the payments.

Figure 16: Mortgage interest rates
Sometimes floating rates are higher, sometimes lower

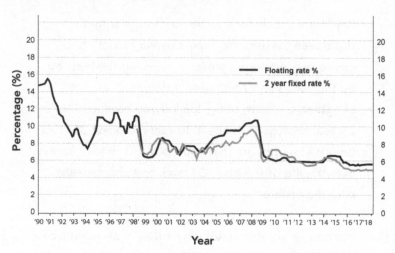

Year

Source: Reserve Bank of NZ (rates offered for new customers)

Figure 16 shows:

- Current mortgage rates are unusually low by historical standards. True, that's partly because inflation is lower than it used to be. But still, inflation has been mainly below 4% since the early 1990s, and yet mortgage interest rates have several times risen above 10% since then.
- Fixed-rate mortgages are not always at lower interest rates than floating mortgages, despite recent history.

There are no guarantees that rates won't go back up above 10%, or that fixed rates will stay below floating rates. Anyone taking out a mortgage needs to keep that in mind.

If you can't cope with a mortgage rate rise

The first thing to do is talk to your mortgage lender. If you talk before you get behind with payments, they are much more likely to accommodate you. Some possible solutions:

- Pay interest only for a while – although sometimes this doesn't reduce payments by very much. And you're making no progress on reducing the loan, so do this for as short a time as possible.
- Lengthen the term of the loan. If you have a 20- or 25-year mortgage, make it 30 years, or even 35. This does mean, though, that you'll pay lots more interest over the life of the loan. Go back to a shorter term later if possible.

The situation is similar if for any other reason you can no longer make mortgage payments. If approached early, a lender may reduce your payments for a while, or offer one of the above alternatives. Whatever the solution, you will end up paying more total interest. But it sure beats a mortgage foreclosure – the forced sale of your house to repay your mortgage.

True tale: Take care with extra borrowing

Says a friend, sadly: 'My elder daughter and her husband bought and sold several houses in succession in the Waikato. Each time they sold for more than they paid, but each succeeding house cost more and involved a higher mortgage.

'Their small business was then severely hit by the global financial crisis and folded. The business had been financed in part by the equity in their house, and they lost both their income and the house when they could no longer pay the mortgage. They now rent in Hamilton.'

Moral: It can be risky to 'borrow against the equity in your home' – which basically means you increase your mortgage to raise money for something, often a business. When people first do it, they are always full of hope and don't imagine things could go wrong. But when bad stuff happens, and you lose your home as well as your dreams, it's pretty rough.

Types of mortgages

Don't skip this bit if you've already got a mortgage. There's a pretty good chance you haven't got the best one for you. If you decide another type would suit you better, your lender may let you switch – although if you have a fixed-term loan you will probably have to wait until the term ends. If the lender makes it difficult to shift, ask another lender if you can move to them, or discuss your situation with a mortgage adviser or mortgage broker.

More on them shortly. But first, the basics.

There are several types of mortgages available. We won't go into the more uncommon choices, like whether you want a reducing (or straight-line) mortgage – in which payments are higher at first but decrease over time as you pay down the loan. Given how high house prices are these days, there would be little demand for that.

But the following are options you should consider.

Fixed or floating interest?

As we've just seen in Figure 16, fixed-rate mortgages tend to be lower than floating these days. But by the time you read this, it could be the other way around.

A fixed rate gives you certainty of payments, at least for the term of the loan – although you could be in for a shock if rates rise and your interest jumps at the end of your term. If you're on a floating rate, your interest would rise more gradually.

A big negative of fixed-rate loans is that there are often penalties if you want to repay the loan early – before the year or five years or whatever is up. You might think, 'That won't happen to me. Where would I get the money from?' But people are sometimes surprised by a redundancy payment, an inheritance, a big win or some other windfall.

Early repayment penalties vary widely, depending on what's happened to interest rates since you got your loan. That's why lenders won't tell you in advance what your penalty will be. They'll give you a formula or something, but it will depend on rate movements, which nobody can accurately predict.

Let's say you have a five-year fixed-rate loan at 5%. Three years into the loan, you want to pay it back.

- If interest rates have risen in the meantime, the lender might not mind if you pay back the loan early. They can then lend out that money at a higher rate. So your penalty might be small or even nothing.
- If interest rates have fallen, the lender really wants to keep your loan going, bringing in what have become really good returns for them. Your penalty in that situation can be huge.

Back in 2008–09, when mortgage interest rates plunged (see Figure 16), many people with fixed-rate mortgages naturally wanted out, so they could move to a much lower rate. But of course the lenders weren't interested, and quoted penalties of many thousands of dollars.

To get a rough idea of what your break fee would be, go to www.tinyurl.com/NZBreakFee. This is a calculator put together by www.interest.co.nz.

However, all is not lost if you want to reduce your mortgage but you face a huge break fee. Many lenders will let you either pay off a certain amount in a lump sum or increase your regular payments up to a certain amount, perhaps 20%. Others will permit extra payments of up to $1,000 a month as long as you commit to making those extra payments until the term of the loan ends.

> **Key message:** If you want to repay a fixed-rate loan faster, don't assume the worst. Ask your lender. And when you renew a fixed-rate mortgage, negotiate for more flexibility in future.

So where are we on the fixed versus floating question? Don't choose just on the basis of interest rates at the time you borrow. That can easily change. Make some of your loan fixed and some floating – perhaps half and half or, if the two rates are very different, two-thirds and one-third.

But do include at least a portion floating, so you can pay it back quickly, no questions asked, if you happen to get a windfall. Also, a floating loan is more flexible. It can be an offset, redrawable or revolving credit mortgage. More about those options shortly.

Which fixed term?

Let's say you're choosing between paying:

- 5% for one year; or
- 6% for five years.

The one-year deal looks better. But by the time you renew it, rates might have risen. Five years down the track you might end up having paid more than if you'd gone with the longer term. On the other hand, if interest rates fall – or don't rise much – you'll wish you had stuck with the shorter term.

It's best to have a portion of the loan each way. Then at least you'll be content with some of your total mortgage.

Traditional, offset, redrawable or revolving credit?

This is where mortgages get interesting. Yes, really. You choose one to go with your lifestyle, how often you get paid, and how strong your willpower is. And in the process, you can pay off the loan faster.

A traditional mortgage

In a traditional mortgage, you make your regular payments – usually fortnightly or monthly. In the meantime, you have money sitting around in your everyday bank account to pay your bills and cover your day-to-day expenses, and hopefully also in a rainy day account or other savings account.

That sitting-around money is usually earning zero or low interest. That means you're *paying*, say, 6% on your mortgage while *earning* very little on your sitting-around money, and even less after tax. No wonder bank profits are so big!

But there are three ways you can turn that around, making things more even between you and your lender. The following types of accounts are not all offered by every lender, but they are around if you look for them. As far as I know, all are available only on floating-rate loans.

An offset mortgage

In an offset mortgage, you pay your mortgage out of your regular bank account. But the balances in all your accounts – and in some cases other accounts owned by family members – are added up and subtracted from the mortgage. So you pay interest only on the lower amount.

None of the accounts earns any interest – but that's probably no big loss.

For example, you have a $300,000 30-year mortgage at 6%, and currently the bank account balances total $5,000. So you pay interest on $300,000 minus $5,000, which is $295,000.

How much difference does that make?

The mortgage calculator at www.sorted.org.nz tells us that if you had a traditional mortgage you would be paying $1,799 a month, and over the life of the loan you would pay a total of $347,515 in interest. (That's more than the mortgage itself – so you pay back more than double what you borrowed. Gulp!)

With the offset, you would pay $1,769 a month, and $341,723 in interest. That amounts to:

- Thirty dollars less a month, which doesn't seem much, but it adds up to $10,800 over the 30 years.
- Nearly $6,000 less interest in total. That's not some theoretical amount, but real dollars in your hand to spend later in life.

What's more, you might decide that with this arrangement you can afford to raise your mortgage payments by the $30 a month. If you add this in, bringing your monthly payments back up to $1,799:

- The total interest you will pay over the life of the loan is more than $24,000 less than with a traditional mortgage. Wow!
- The 30 years to pay off the loan has dropped a little to 29 years. One more year of mortgage freedom is worth something.

A redrawable mortgage
In a redrawable mortgage, you have a separate bank account for your mortgage, and deposit your mortgage payments into it. At any time you can put in more money – either as a lump sum or bigger regular payments. The big plus is that you can go back to the original minimum payment at any time, and you can take out any of the 'overpaid' money if you find you need it.

By parking money in the account for a period, you reduce your balance for a while, and hence your interest payments.

A revolving credit mortgage

In a revolving credit mortgage, your mortgage is part of your everyday account, so it may have a balance of, say, minus $500,000, which can look alarming at first. All your income is deposited into that account, and all your bills paid out of it. In the meantime, that income is credited against the mortgage. The mortgage balance is therefore lower, so you pay less interest.

At any time you can increase your borrowing again – in some cases up to the original limit, although some lenders have a reducing limit, which forces you to pay down the loan over the years.

The idea of a revolving credit mortgage is that, over time, you have more money going into the account than coming out again, so your mortgage balance – the negative value of the account – decreases, finally to nothing.

Revolving credit loans work particularly well for self-employed people with lumpy incomes – sometimes large sums that are used only gradually over several months. They can make good use of their money before it is gradually spent. It can also work well if you plan to renovate your home, as you can withdraw a large sum at any time without having to apply.

I had a revolving credit mortgage for years, and it worked well. I regarded it as a bit of a game to get income into the account as fast as possible and put all bills on automatic payment on the last possible day.

However, if you're not disciplined about getting rid of

your mortgage, this type of loan might not be for you. You might be too tempted to withdraw money from the account – effectively adding to your mortgage – for a holiday or a shopping splurge.

A personality test: Do you always pay off your credit card in full each month? Do you generally spend less than you earn? If yes, you're probably a good candidate for a revolving credit mortgage.

Figure 17: Three clever types of mortgages

	How it works	Mortgage interest calculated on ...	Pluses and minuses
Offset	You and family use normal bank accounts.	... mortgage balance minus money in your (and perhaps family) bank accounts.	All your sitting-around money is reducing your mortgage interest.
Redrawable	Put spare money into mortgage account. Can withdraw that money at any time.	... mortgage balance – which is lower because you have parked money in that account.	Not all your sitting-around money is being used. Easy access to extra deposits if needed.
Revolving credit	Mortgage is part of everyday bank account with big negative balance. All income comes into this account, and bills paid out of it.	... mortgage balance – which is lower because your sitting-around money and any other deposits have reduced it.	All your sitting-around money is reducing your mortgage interest. Can borrow more if needed, but requires self-discipline.

Basically, all three of these types of mortgages work in much the same way. The set-ups are different, but with all of them you make use of your sitting-around money to pay less interest. The interest is calculated daily, so even if you park money in an account for a few days it all helps.

With less money being wasted on interest, more can go into reducing the principal – the amount you borrowed in the first place. So you end up paying off the loan faster.

Note that it might cost you more to set up an offset, redrawable or revolving credit mortgage than a traditional loan, and some lenders charge a monthly fee. But in most cases the advantages more than make up for that.

A great place for rainy day money

If you have an offset, redrawable or revolving credit mortgage, keep your rainy day money in your bank account, so that it's keeping down the mortgage balance until you need it.

Monthly or fortnightly payments?

Every now and then you hear someone say that you can cut the amount of interest you pay – and the time it takes to pay off your mortgage – by simply switching from monthly payments of, say, $1,000 to fortnightly payments of $500, half the amount. They sometimes present the idea as some kind of clever trick.

But there's no magic. While there are, of course, 12 months in a year, there are not twice as many fortnights, but 26. So you make extra payments each year. Of course you'll pay the mortgage off faster.

Still, fortnightly payments might suit you better than monthly if you are paid fortnightly. The downside is that if you have other payments that are monthly, such as electricity or phone bills, and you're on a tight budget, it can wreak havoc in the couple of months each year when there are three rather than two fortnightly mortgage payments.

Shopping for a mortgage

Your first step is to look at a table of current mortgage rates. A good source is www.interest.co.nz, or you can look each week to the right of my *Weekend Herald* column, in the business section. That will give you an idea of what's out there.

Don't confine yourself to your own bank. There's no reason why you can't get a mortgage from a different lender.

But rather than just looking at who offers the lowest rates today, it's better to look at long-term trends. After all, today's lowest mortgage provider might raise its rates tomorrow. To compare different banks' rates since 2002, go to www.tinyurl.com/NZMortgageRates.

Then, to get an idea of what your monthly or fortnightly payments would be with a certain mortgage, I recommend the mortgage calculator on www.sorted.org.nz, although there are many others online.

A good next step is probably to go to an independent mortgage adviser or mortgage broker. They will help you find a suitable loan, and they know things like which lenders are more sympathetic if you have a bad credit record or low income.

You don't pay the adviser, and they should get you as good an interest rate as you could on your own. But, as in any other situation when somebody is offering you something free, you should ask what's in it for them. In this case, if the mortgage adviser organises a loan for you, that lender pays the adviser commission.

This can be a worry. If one lender pays more than another, the adviser may tend to favour them. Also, mortgage advisers don't deal with every lender. So it's important to ask them which lenders they're not considering, and also how much commission they get from the different lenders.

This might feel like an awkward conversation, but it's your money at stake. Just say I told you to ask! If they are not happy to answer, that in itself should tell you something. Keep in mind what they tell you, and check that you can't get a better deal from a lender they don't work with.

But I don't want to be too negative. A good mortgage adviser knows lots about the different bells and whistles that lenders offer and how to approach the lenders. And if they want to keep a good reputation, they'll do their best for you.

It was actually a mortgage adviser who gave me the following tip: *don't automatically go for a 30-year mortgage*. Banks usually suggest 30 years, the adviser says, but that may be because they get more interest out of a longer-term loan.

Let's look again at our $300,000 mortgage at 6%:

- Over 30 years, you would pay $1,799 a month and total interest of $347,500.
- Over 25 years, you would pay $1,933 a month and total interest of $279,900.
- Over 20 years, you would pay $2,149 a month and total interest of $215,800.

Take a close look at those numbers. Moving from 30 to 25 years you pay just $134 more per month. And what do you get for that? More than $67,000 off your interest bill. And you're mortgage-free five years earlier.

What if you go the whole hog, to a 20-year mortgage? Sure, you have to pay $350 more a month than on a 30-year loan. But you're more than $131,000 better off. And you're mortgage-free a whole decade earlier.

On a mortgage twice as big – $600,000 – double the figures above.

True tale: Never give up

Back on page 114, under 'Champion savers', I wrote about a woman who saved for a house while earning $30,000 a year. How did she get a mortgage on such a low income? Persistence. She had a 75% deposit when she approached several banks for a loan. Three said no, but one said yes.

With the loan, she bought a two-bedroom Auckland house for $500,000. She's paying off the mortgage at $600 per month – almost certainly less than the rent she had been paying.

Moral: Don't get discouraged. Not all lenders are the same.

Reducing a mortgage

We're not talking here about making the regular minimum payments you must make on most mortgages. It goes without saying that you should do that. And, as I said above, if you can't it's essential that you discuss that with the lender.

In most cases, though, people make regular mortgage payments year in year out until the loan is paid off. But –

as teachers used to say on our school reports – we could do better.

I read recently that only 13% of New Zealanders with mortgages say they can't afford to pay more than the minimum mortgage payments. That means the rest – quite likely including you – could stretch themselves further. It's a super idea.

Getting rid of your mortgage means more than just no longer having to make payments – although that's pretty good.

It also means you have guaranteed accommodation, no matter what happens to house prices or your financial situation. And should you get into financial trouble – or need money to help out family members or invest in your daughter's new hi-tech business – you will probably be able to borrow back against the house. Without a mortgage, you're also in a much better position to take on higher-risk, higher-return investments.

Apparently, the average New Zealander clears their mortgage at age 60. Set a goal to do it younger. (See 'Setting a goal' on page 26.)

Nearly always with a floating-rate loan the lender will accept higher payments. As noted above, that might not be the case with a fixed loan, although you should always ask. If your request gets you nowhere, wait until the end of the term and then make part of the loan floating.

There are various ways to pay down a mortgage faster:

- The easiest way: When interest rates fall on a floating-rate loan, simply continue with the old payments. This is likely to happen several times in the course of a mortgage, and it's a great opportunity.
- Go to the lender and renegotiate a shorter term. You might have started out with a 30-year loan but after a

while – perhaps after a few pay rises – you realise you could cope with a 20- or 25-year loan.

- If you have an offset, redrawable or revolving credit loan, you can simply hold more money in your bank account. That will be subtracted from the mortgage balance, and so has the same effect as reducing the balance.
- Switch from monthly payments to fortnightly payments of half the monthly amount. But see the note of caution a few pages back.

Let's look at an example of the first option – maintaining your payments when the interest rate drops. On our $300,000 30-year loan, at 6% you pay $1,799 a month. If interest rates drop to 5.5%, you pay $1,703 a month. But if you keep the payments at the old $1,799, you will pay up to $79,000 less interest and pay off the loan up to three years earlier – depending on how far through the 30 years you are. Nice!

To do your own calculations, go to the mortgage calculator on www.sorted.org.nz. Play around with it. See what happens when you increase your repayments.

Let me repeat what I said before: *the interest savings are real dollars – extra money you'll have.* Think what you could do with $79,000 more in retirement. Actually, it will be more than that, because in the meantime it will have grown through compounding returns.

Someone once said, 'Rich people never know the satisfaction of making that last mortgage payment.' And it *is* a great feeling. By all means celebrate, perhaps blowing what would have been your next mortgage payment on a treat.

After that, it's time to get into serious retirement saving with the money that used to go into mortgage payments. If you've paid off the mortgage faster, you've got that many more years to build up a decent sum with which to have a great retirement.

True tale: A narrow focus

'I'm the trustee of someone's small family trust,' says a friend of mine. 'They still had a mortgage over their house, held in the trust, and they got an inheritance of about $1 million. Somehow they met a personal financial adviser from a big well-known firm, who wanted to pitch to put the $1 million in a non-KiwiSaver balanced fund. The couple asked me to come to the pitch.'

My friend realised that the return on the balanced fund, after tax and fees, was about three percentage points less than the mortgage interest they were paying. So they would be much better off using the money to pay down the mortgage.

'The adviser was looking at the $1 million in isolation, ignoring the rest of the portfolio,' says my friend. He talked the couple out of taking the adviser's advice.

> **Moral:** There are three morals here – give priority to reducing a mortgage (with the exception of contributing to KiwiSaver); consider your whole range of investments and debts; and beware of advisers who are overly keen on investing your money – probably because they will get commission for it. (More on that shortly, in 'Do you need personal financial advice?', page 271.)

Selling a home

Depending on why you are selling your home, you might not have a lot of time to prepare it for sale. But it's a really good idea to spend a few weeks smartening the place up. I've heard too many stories of people selling their house as is, only to hear within a year that the buyer spent, say, $50,000 on some clever improvements and resold the house for $200,000 or $300,000 more than they bought it for. Ouch!

Pay particular attention to the first impression buyers will get – whether that be your letterbox (which they'll be looking for to check they are at the right house) or the gate, garden and front door. Think like a buyer. We've all looked at houses and been put off before we even entered the place. Also consider getting the house painted. It doesn't cost a great deal to make a house look much smarter.

Experts say that kitchens and bathrooms can make or break a sale, so consider putting in a new kitchen or bathroom. If the old one is less than, say, 20 years old, it may not be worth it, but spending the same amount replacing a tired 50-year-old kitchen or bathroom is likely to pay off. Another feature that apparently helps to sell a house is adding a deck – although not every place lends itself to that.

These days, quite a few houses for sale are 'staged', with a company coming in and adding flash furniture, art and so on. You might want to hire an expert, or you can read a few online articles and do it yourself.

A major point the companies make is to 'declutter'. If you've got lots of stuff around the house, put it in cartons at a friend's place. And at the very least, buy a few bright cushions to liven up the living room or a couple of mats to cover carpet stains.

By the way, home buyers should be aware of this. If you're getting serious about buying a house, lift the rugs, and try to look beyond the staging!

Real estate agents' commissions

You don't have to use an agent to sell your home. It's getting easier, with the internet, to get the word out about your wonderful property, and you can find online support for selling on your own, often called 'selling privately'. Start with the Citizens Advice Bureau website, which lists pros and cons of private sales.

I've sold my own house once, in Chicago. The most difficult part was negotiating with two keen buyers. But in retrospect I could have hired someone, perhaps a lawyer, to do the negotiations for much less than real estate commission. The rest – advertising and running open homes – wasn't so difficult. Some of you might want to give it a go.

But it takes time, effort and research. Probably most people prefer to hire an expert.

While a lot of the big real estate companies charge similar sales commissions, there are some that are considerably cheaper.

It's important to know, too, that you can negotiate commissions. This works especially well in a slower property market, where agents are extra keen to get your listing.

I object to the way most NZ real estate agents structure their commissions. It means that they have little incentive to get the best price for you. But you can always propose a different, fairer structure. An example is probably the best way to show this:

Let's say you meet with three or four agents to discuss listing your house. Get in writing how much they expect you'll get for the house. Then ask how their commission is structured.

It will probably be something like: 3.95% of the first $200,000 (which comes to $7,900) plus 2% of the rest. If the expected price is $700,000, the commission would be $7,900 plus $10,000, which is $17,900.

When you've chosen your agent, tell them you would like to structure the commission as shown in Figure 18.

By following Figure 18, if they sell at the expected $700,000, they will get the same $17,900.

If they sell for more, for every dollar over $700,000 they get 10% extra. Say they did brilliantly and you sold for $800,000. They would get $17,900 plus 10% of $100,000, which is $10,000. Their total commission would be a fat $27,900. You pay a lot more, but you don't mind, because you got such a good price.

Under the standard formula they would have got $17,900 plus just 2% of $100,000, which is $2,000 – bringing their total to just $19,900. That's not much more for them, after they did so well, especially given that part of the agent's commission goes to their firm. Why would they bother to put much extra effort into getting you a high price?

But if they sell for less than $700,000, for every dollar under that price they get 10% less. Say the sale price ended

Figure 18: Our example of a fairer deal in real estate commission

Sale price	Standard commission	A fairer deal
The expected $700,000	$17,900	$17,900
A really good $800,000	$19,900	$27,900
A really disappointing $600,000	$15,900	$7,900

up being only $600,000. They would get $17,900 *minus* 10% of the $100,000 shortfall. That's $17,900 minus $10,000, or just $7,900.

Under the standard formula it would have been $17,900 minus $2,000 – a total of $15,900. They did poorly, but they would have got much the same commission as if they had done well.

Point out how much more they will get if they do well for you, while acknowledging that if they do badly they will get a lot less.

Some agents will baulk at this. It's an interesting test, actually, of how confident they really are that they will get you $700,000. Agents often overestimate the price, in the hope you will list with them.

To encourage them, consider offering a bonus of, say, $1,000 over and above their commission, at whatever price they get. If the agent still won't go along with it, ask another one you met.

I've successfully used this structure twice. Once we sold for way less than we had hoped – and the agent had indicated – but it was some consolation to know we weren't paying out many thousands for a job poorly done. The other time we sold at about the expected price.

On another occasion, though, none of the agents working in that suburb would go along with my proposal. Collusion? Who knows? It was worth a try.

Other issues when choosing an agent

When you're discussing commissions with agents, the companies that charge more will tell you that you pay for quality, but I'm not sure that's necessarily true.

How do you tell quality? Ask the agents for written info on recent houses they have sold, including their price expectations and what they sold the properties for.

Get details on how they plan to market your property, and how much you'll have to pay for the marketing. Apparently most house buyers these days first spot a property online, so make sure the online marketing is done well – including perhaps Trade Me, Facebook and Google advertising.

Also, of course, ask your friends and neighbours for recommendations. And – importantly – check the public register on the Real Estate Authority website, www.rea.govt. nz, to make sure the agent is licensed. The register will also tell you whether there is any 'disciplinary history' over the past three years for that agent – in other words, whether there have been any complaints upheld against them.

It's not about the car

Some people say you can judge a real estate agent by their car. If it's expensive, they must be doing well, which suggests they are good at their job. Then again, it might suggest their commissions are too high! Or perhaps they've run up a huge debt to buy the flash car. Remember *The Millionaire Next Door*? Ignore the car, and take note of what they say they will do for you – in writing. Ditto expensive clothes.

Tips for sellers

- Before you even talk to agents, pay for a professional valuation of your property. That gives you power when negotiating with agents or buyers if they're talking too low a price. It also signals when an agent may be suggesting too high a price when they first meet you.

- While agents are supposed to be getting you the best price, they have a big incentive to sell fast and move on to the next property, especially under the usual commission structure discussed above. *Don't be pressured to accept a low offer, especially early on.*

- Usually agents' contracts are for 60 or 90 days. Go for 60 or perhaps less. If the property hasn't sold at the end of the contract period, you might want to try a different agent. Take note, though, of a warning from Consumer NZ. Some contracts say you have to pay the first agent if a buyer who saw the property while that agent was listing it comes back and makes an offer via a second agent. You could find yourself paying commissions to both. Don't sign any contract that requires you to pay a commission once the contract has expired.

- You can renegotiate the agent's commission at any time. Let's say a buyer's final offer is less than you are willing to take. Ask the agent if they will reduce their commission, so you end up with a bit more. They might agree, just to get the sale.

Step ? check

Have you:

- ❏ Decided whether you want to own a home?
- ❏ If yes: thought about options – a boat, a tiny house, buying with friends, being a renter-landlord?

❑ Done your homework before buying – see our list?

❑ Looked into mortgage choices?

If you already own a home, have you:

❑ Considered changing your mortgage?

❑ Set up a plan to pay off the mortgage faster?

If you want to sell, have you:

❑ Put effort into making the house look great, picking an agent and negotiating commission?

Reward

Chocolates, cheese or flowers; or a 'me day' with a walk, book, time with family, being creative; or donating to a charity, or anything else that makes you smile.

What's next? If you want help with your money, let's get good help.

ONE MORE THING: DO YOU NEED PERSONAL FINANCIAL ADVICE?

In which we ...

- Consider whether you need an adviser
- Raise doubts about whether some will really act in your interests
- Narrow down the options
- Decide what to ask them by email ...
- ... And then in person

If you have a complex financial situation, you may want to hire a financial adviser. They're a very mixed bag, though, so here are some tips on how to find a competent one.

A good adviser will consider everything – your debts and investments, when you want to spend your savings, and your tolerance for risk. They will love the fact that you've read this book, because you'll understand why they are making their recommendations and will ask good questions about their approach. (If they don't welcome challenging questions, they are not a good adviser.)

Note that I said 'hire' an adviser. There are, unfortunately, still financial advisers operating in New Zealand who offer 'free' advice. Why do they do it? When they put your money into certain investments, the companies that provide those investments give them commissions. Or they might work for a company that provides investment products and they receive bonuses or similar for investing your money in their company's products.

People in these situations sometimes protest that they don't necessarily advise their clients to invest in the products that give the advisers the best deal. But how can you be confident they have your best interests at heart?

Look at it this way: How would you feel if you found out that your doctor prescribed a certain drug for you, knowing that another drug would do a better job, but the company that makes the first drug was giving the doctor a bigger reward? If you go with an adviser who is rewarded by someone else, rather than you, there's a big chance you'll end up in investments that may be okay, but are not the best ones for you. Andrew Hubbard of the CAB (Citizens Advice Bureau) said recently, 'Just as there's no such thing as a free lunch, there's definitely no such thing as free financial advice. And bad advice is potentially worse than no advice at all.'

Want a good financial adviser? Pay for it.

Here come the robots

The exception to the 'pay for it' rule is getting simple advice online from chatbots and robo-advisers.

It's becoming increasingly likely that we'll get our financial advice from these creatures. Many KiwiSaver providers are already offering some advice using artificial intelligence (AI), or soon will be. In particular, they're looking at helping people work out:

- which KiwiSaver fund they should be in;
- whether they're on the right track with their long- or short-term savings, and if not what to do about it; or,
- what to do with their KiwiSaver savings when they reach 65.

Some will also offer guidance during market turbulence.

We will, of course, need to always be aware who is providing the robo-advice. I expect some providers will quite openly deal only with their own products, but others may do it more subtly. And some may 'cheat' by using assumptions about returns that are too high. It's preferable to use tools from an independent source, such as the Commission for Financial Capability.

In some ways I think AI will be better than humans. A good financial robo-adviser will ask all the important questions, take into account at least some of your circumstances and make the best decisions it can for you, whereas a human adviser might slip up sometimes.

But of course there'll be limits. If the robo-adviser can't cope with your complex question, you might be moved on to a flesh-and-blood adviser. At that point, you might want to say, 'Thanks but no thanks,' and choose your own adviser.

How to find some possible advisers

Many financial advisers are good at marketing themselves. They might recruit you at a free seminar or via a free phone discussion. They might even charge for the seminar or discussion so it doesn't look dodgy. I'm not saying every financial adviser who reaches out to the public is suspect, but be wary.

Nor is it a great idea to go with the recommendation of a friend or relative. I've heard stories of people being very happy with their nice adviser – who remembers their birthday – only to discover that their investments are too undiversified, or riskier than they thought and have gone wobbly.

So how *do* you find someone good?

Some years ago I decided I should do more than just tell people to shop around. So I started the Info on Advisers page on my website, www.maryholm.com. The page explains why it's important to go with an adviser who charges you fees. Then I list such advisers.

When I started this page, some people said I wouldn't find many, and the list numbered only about a dozen firms. But word has got out, and there are now more than 50 firms on the list. (Any fee-charging firms out there that are not on the list, feel free to contact me.) To be there, every adviser has to agree in writing to the following:

- 'I guarantee that when I give any new client investment advice or help them to make any investments, the only money or other consideration I receive is explicitly stated fees that I charge the client. Any commissions or other considerations I receive from financial firms or others are passed on in full to the client.'

- 'I promise to give any clients who request it a signed letter that says, "I truly believe I have given you the best advice I can, having considered a wide range of products, and that I have told you about all real or potential conflicts of interest."'

The advisers also have to say that they give advice on all types of investments, including general advice about property. For example, the adviser could help a client weigh up whether to invest in rental property versus investing in a share fund.

Along with contact details, the list includes a minimum initial investment amount for each firm. Many have no minimum, and for some this is not applicable because they don't actually make investments for you, but just tell you where they think you should invest. But for some the minimum is as high as $500,000.

Two important notes about the list:

- I've never met most of the advisers, and know little about them other than that they have agreed to the provisions above. So I am not recommending them – I'm just saying *a good place to start is with advisers who charge fees*. Nor am I in a position to check whether what they say is true. I just encourage readers to let me know if you are ever worried about how one of these advisers operates.
- I'm running this list as a labour of love. Some advisers say I should charge them to be on the list. After all, they pick up clients that way. But readers might then think I'm endorsing the advisers or letting marginal advisers onto the list so I get more money. So it's all free.

Have a look through the list, read the websites of several and pick some that appeal. Check the advisers' qualifications. If I were you, I would want someone with a relevant degree, preferably in finance, although any business or commerce degree is probably a good sign. We expect our doctors, lawyers, accountants and other professionals to have been to university. If an adviser doesn't list their qualifications, you can be pretty sure they don't have very good ones.

Within a firm that looks good, read about the individual advisers. Some might sound more like your sort of person than others.

A lighter look at advisers

Fans of the funny American TV show *Last Week Tonight with John Oliver* will enjoy his 22-minute June 2016 episode on money, at www.tinyurl.com/OliverMoney

Amidst the humour, Oliver points out that many financial advisers are poorly qualified and also motivated not to put your interests first.

He also makes three other basic points that you will by now know inside out:

- Start saving now.
- High fees make a huge difference to how fast your savings grow.
- Use low-fee index funds, not active funds.

Questions to ask advisers

The next step is to email questions to several advisers, so you have their replies in writing. Briefly describe your situation and what you want help with – whether it's just how to invest an inheritance or a review of your whole financial situation, including such things as wills.

Then ask them to say, briefly, how they would help you. Don't let them fob you off by saying they will tell you when they meet you. You want a broad outline of how they go about their work.

Some questions you would otherwise ask have been taken care of in the promises they made to get on my website, but it would be a good idea to ask them again, in your own words.

I would also ask how they charge – by the hour, a flat fee, or a percentage of your investments – and what their rates are. And ask if they charge an annual monitoring fee, how much it is, and what they do for it. Such fees can be rip-offs, if the adviser doesn't do much. But a reasonable price for an annual review might be money well spent.

Obviously, once you've questioned several advisers you'll get an idea of the fee range. Don't necessarily cross off those with the highest fees, but ask them, if you meet them, why their fees are higher than other advisers' fees.

If an adviser doesn't reply to your email reasonably promptly, I would give them a miss. Similarly, if they pussyfoot around about their fees. They won't be able to give you an estimate without meeting you, but they should be upfront about their rates.

Meet the candidates for the job of advising you

Nearly all the advisers on my list say they will give you a free initial meeting, although a few named ones offer just a free initial phone conversation. Some limit the free meeting to half an hour, so ask first if there's a time limit.

I strongly advise you to take up this opportunity with three or four of them. And while it might seem as if they are interviewing you, because they will ask you questions, I hope you can regard this as you interviewing them. Remember, they will be working for you.

At this stage, ask them to estimate their fees for what you want them to do. Then follow that up with an email asking them to confirm that estimate. I've heard of people being shocked at the size of some advisers' fees. You should have a good idea before you start.

Tip: A good adviser who wants the best for you will ask about your debts as well as your savings – and will suggest you pay off high-interest debt before doing anything else. They will also ask about your KiwiSaver membership and what sort of fund you are in. This is stuff that might not generate them much income, but is highly important to you.

Choose an adviser you trust who appears to be on your wavelength and seems to know what they are talking about. That doesn't mean they throw financial jargon at you. It's really important that you understand everything they say.

It's a bit like choosing a doctor. In the olden days, we used to just blindly accept what our doctors told us. These days most of us like to understand how they are treating us and why. Same goes for our finances.

The inexpert 'experts'

When a person is seeking advice on an investment or other financial issue, I often hear people say, 'Ask Fred – he's an accountant (or a lawyer or a businessman). He'll know.' He probably won't – but that might not stop him from expressing his opinion.

Over the years I've seen this happen way too often. There's no doubt that some accountants, lawyers and business people understand markets and are good advisers on money matters. But many seem reluctant to explain that this is not their area of expertise, and then go on to give plain bad advice. While some financial advisers don't give good advice either, if you go through the process above, you should find one who does.

Financial adviser check

Have you:

- ❏ Decided whether to go down the adviser track?
- ❏ Looked through the list of fee-charging advisers?
- ❏ Drawn up a list of questions to ask by email?
- ❏ Interviewed several before choosing one?

Reward

Chocolates, cheese or flowers; or a 'me day' with a walk, book, time with family, being creative; or donating to a charity, or anything else that makes you smile.

ON HAPPINESS

Remember back at the start of this book, when I was telling you about how I asked my students to rate people they knew on wealth and happiness? After we looked at whether the students saw a correlation between the two, I asked them to think about the people they had given their highest and lowest happiness ratings to. What was it that made them seem so happy or unhappy?

The students came up with all sorts of replies – to do with health, family relationships, how hard people work, helping others, the ability to travel, social circles and so on. Some responses were about personalities – whether people are optimistic and whether they feel gratitude and appreciation.

As the students called out their replies, I wrote them on the blackboard in two lists. At the end, I asked why I had some replies in one list, and some in the other. Someone always realised quite quickly. The items in the shorter list cost money. The items in the longer list did not. It became pretty clear that money doesn't seem to be the main source of contentment.

We then looked at another pair of lists, as compiled by Nick Powdthavee in *The Happiness Equation*, as follows:

- Jobs with the lowest job satisfaction: roofers, waiters/servers, labourers (except construction), bartenders, hand packers and packagers etc.
- Jobs with the highest job satisfaction: clergy, physiotherapists, firefighters, education administrators, painters and sculptors etc, teachers, authors, psychologists, special education teachers, operating engineers.

'What can we learn from this?' I asked the students. Once again, a bright spark worked it out. Most of the highly satisfying jobs involved creativity or significant interactions with people. What they didn't involve was particularly high pay. Where were the doctors, lawyers, accountants and chief executives?

The students and I also discussed research on big winners in lotteries. While some winners seemed to be happy, others were miserable. How could you trust the sincerity of any new friend you made? For many winners, a year later they were about as happy or unhappy as they had been before their big win. As Powdthavee said, people tend to adapt to good and bad things – getting married, or the death of a loved one – faster than they expect to.

Then we turned to spending, and research that finds you're likely to be happier if you:

- Buy experiences instead of things. Things get old, but experiences – concerts and shows, being out in the wilderness, travel, or just spending time with friends – stay shiny in your memory.
- Buy many small pleasures instead of a few big ones.

- Pay now and consume later. Anticipation is part of happiness. Also, you enjoy it more when you know the bill is already paid.
- Spend on others instead of yourself.

I've got no idea how many of the students were convinced by their reading and the discussion. But I like to think they walked away at least pondering whether the common drive to accumulate more wealth is what life is all about.

Beyond a certain point ...

Recent research by Andrew T. Jebb, Louis Tay, Ed Diener & Shigehiro Oishi, published in 2018 in the journal *Nature Human Behaviour*, finds that – on average – happiness seems to actually decline beyond a certain income.

The study was based on a global survey of 1.7 million people. The researchers looked at what they called 'subjective wellbeing', which is made up of:

- Life evaluation. Participants were asked to imagine a ladder with steps labelled 0 to 10. Zero represents the 'worst possible life', and 10 is the 'best possible life'. They had to decide which step they personally stand on at the present time.
- Affective wellbeing. People were asked whether they had experienced certain emotional states for much of the day yesterday. For 'positive affect', the emotional states were happiness, enjoyment and smiling/ laughter. For 'negative affect', the emotional states were stress, worry and sadness.

Results differed for different regions. The income level at which life evaluation peaked in Australia and New Zealand was about NZ$184,000 for a single-income household – and higher for larger households.

But turning to affective wellbeing, the peak income level for our region was much lower – around NZ$73,000.

It's hard to know what to make of that big difference – which applied across all regions. Rather than dwelling on the details, let's just say that getting richer could in some cases be harmful to your happiness.

The researchers made two particularly interesting observations. The first was that if the income of a person earning at the peak level – say $73,000 – was suddenly doubled, they might well feel happier at first. That's not what the research is about. Rather, it's showing that 'groups at the higher income are no happier than groups at the lower initial income'.

The fact that higher-income people in fact seemed somewhat less happy 'may speak to the reality of the "hedonic treadmill" – the well-studied phenomenon that happiness levels tend to return to a relatively constant baseline amidst various life events and circumstances'.

See what I said above about lottery winners!

It's important to note, too, that the research is looking at averages. Some individuals will be happier as their income climbs to billions of dollars, while others need little money to be very happy.

The second observation made by the researchers was that presumably it's not the higher incomes themselves that make people less happy, 'but the costs associated with them. High incomes are usually accompanied by high demands (time, workload, responsibility and so on) that might also limit opportunities for positive experiences (for example, leisure activities).

'Additional factors may play a role as well, such as an increase in materialistic values, additional material aspirations that may go unfulfilled, increased social comparisons or other life changes in reaction to greater income (for example, more children or living in more expensive neighbourhoods). Importantly, the ill effects of the highest incomes may not just be present when one's maximum income is finally reached, but could also occur in the process of its attainment.'

It's worth pondering.

What makes New Zealanders happy?

Over several years, up until 2014, the market research company UMR did research on what makes New Zealanders aged 18 and older happy. The findings were fairly similar year after year, so I suppose we can expect they would be much the same now.

Around 30% of the population gave themselves 9 out of 10 or 10 out of 10 for happiness. The scores were somewhat higher for women than men.

But the clearest difference was age. Our graph shows a strong trend. People become less and less happy as they head into their forties and fifties, but then a miracle occurs! They get markedly happier from then on, with the 75-plusers being happiest of all.

It was funny when I showed Figure 19 to my university students, most of whom were in their late teens. They expected people to get less and less happy as they got older, perhaps because they watched their parents wilt as mortgages and difficult teens – the students themselves! – took their toll.

Percentage of 'very happy' people in each age group

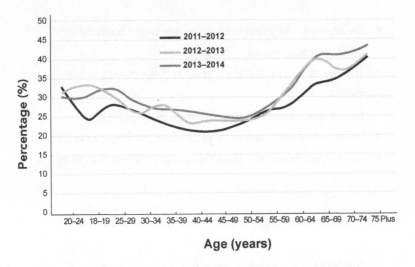

Source: UMR research

But the students thought old people would be unhappier still. I just smiled.

The survey's findings on income are puzzling. They seem to contradict other research to some extent, in that the group with the highest happiness score was the highest income group. But those on low incomes came second, being happier than those in the middle. Maybe age is what's really driving those results. Older people tend to be on higher incomes, and younger people on lower incomes.

One striking – and encouraging – result was New Zealanders' responses to the question: 'Is your job something you do to pay the bills and you would take another one if the pay was better, or is your job more of a calling that you really enjoy and feel is important?' Nearly two-thirds – 65% – said their job was a calling, with only 30% saying they worked just to pay the bills.

What else? The five factors most strongly associated with high scores for happiness were:

- being very satisfied with your work–life balance (55% of this group are very happy);
- being very satisfied with your achievements in life (53%);
- being very involved in the community (42%);
- being very satisfied with your physical fitness (41%);
- being politically on what the survey called the 'firm right' (40%).

Other factors with some correlation to happiness were:

- feeling that you have excellent control over your life;
- being very satisfied with your weight;
- knowing your neighbours very well.

What can we learn from this? You can't do much about your age or gender. But if your job is not your calling, you might want to change that.

Other steps you might want to consider include: changing your work–life balance, increasing your community involvement and neighbourliness, or working on your fitness and weight. I'm not sure, though, that an artificially imposed move to the right wing of politics would work!

The joys of spring

Does your happiness change with the seasons? UMR looked at this over several years and found that happiness rises from the start of the year until March, and then falls to its lowest point in July, in the depths of winter.

But as July ends, our happiness swings back up, reaching its highest point of the year in September. It stays about the same through spring, but falls slightly heading into December and the Christmas rush. All quite predictable when you come to think about it.

Money, couples and family relationships

One thing that wasn't covered in the UMR surveys, but came up frequently when the students talked about why they scored people as happy or unhappy, was relationships between couples and among family members. And money certainly plays a role in this, although more money doesn't necessarily mean more harmony.

Relationship Services reports that financial differences are the biggest reason for relationship breakdown. They recommend that couples talk about their attitudes to money, preferably before problems arise. But if they've already arisen in your relationship, it's not too late! Start by asking one another how money was dealt with when each of you was growing up.

The experts point out that sometimes a relationship difficulty is not really so much about money as about how financial decisions are made. It's a good idea to agree on this.

Often problems surface around shopping. Note that research at Stanford University found that 'contrary to popular opinion, nearly as many men as women experience compulsive buying disorder, a condition marked by binge buying and subsequent financial hardship'.

Moving beyond couples to the broader family, if parents are giving more financial support to one adult child than to his or her siblings, it's often a good idea to discuss this with the others to avoid accusations of favouritism. The siblings may agree that one of them needs extra help, perhaps because of bad luck or ill health. One possible solution: uneven treatment may be evened up later with provisions in a will.

Happier than most other countries

How do New Zealanders compare with the rest of the developed world on happiness?

The OECD (Organisation for Economic Co-operation and Development), which has 38 member countries including us, puts together a Better Life Index, which is a bit of an eye-opener.

> **Key message:** It seems that New Zealanders' happiness might be less tied up with income than in many other countries.

The OECD looks at 11 wellbeing factors. New Zealand's highest score is for health (we're first out of 38, with a score of 9.6 on a scale of 1 to 10), and our second highest score is for our general satisfaction with life (9.1).

Meanwhile, our lowest score is for income (3.5). We have below average household disposable (after-tax) income, and below average household wealth.

Other findings:

- We get a high score for community (95% of people believe that they know someone they could rely on in a time of need, compared with 89% across the OECD).

- We also do well on environmental quality (which measures air pollution, water quality and so on).
- We're pretty good on jobs, but not so good on work–life balance.
- We're above average for civic engagement (voter turnout etc), housing, education and skills.
- But – somewhat surprisingly – we're below average for personal security (feeling safe walking alone at night, and the murder rate).

To check out this fascinating research, and to see where New Zealand ranks compared with any other country or all of them, go to www.oecdbetterlifeindex.org. You can also create your own index on this intriguing website, giving more importance to some factors and less to others, and check out gender differences.

Where do you rank on the world's rich list?

Feeling hard done by? Go to www.globalrichlist.com. By answering a couple of questions about your income, or your wealth, you can find out roughly where you rank in the world. You might be surprised.

Last words on happiness

The *Harvard Business Review* put it this way: 'People who make progress every day toward something they care about report being satisfied and fulfilled.'

American broadcaster Andy Rooney put it *this* way: 'Everyone wants to live on top of the mountain, but all the happiness and growth occurs while you're climbing it.'

And Chris Anderson, head of TED, wrote in his book *TED Talks, The Official TED Guide to Public Speaking*: 'We're strange creatures, we humans. At one level we just want to eat, drink, play, and acquire more stuff. But life on the hedonic treadmill is ultimately dissatisfying. A beautiful remedy is to hop off it and instead begin pursuing an idea that's bigger than you are.'

Meanwhile, the UK Government's Foresight Programme offers these Five Pointers for Lifelong Wellbeing:

1. Connect with people around you.
2. Be active – do physical activity that suits you.
3. Be curious – watch for the beautiful or unusual.
4. Keep learning – anything. It might be a musical instrument, or how to cook.
5. Give – to a friend or a stranger. Volunteer.

What's not on the list?

Useful links and websites

Throughout this book you'll see links that start 'www.tinyurl.com'. That's not the name of the website! I use tinyurl to make links much shorter than they really are, so it's easier for you to type them in.

Step 2: Kill off high-interest debt
To send a message to yourself at a future date: www.futureme.org
To see the effect of paying off a credit card faster: Debt Calculator on www.sorted.org.nz
Three-minute TED talk on changing a habit: www.tinyurl.com/30DaysTED
Help with controlling your spending: FinCap (previously called the National Building Financial Capability Charitable Trust): www.fincap.org.nz
KiwiSaver contributions holiday: www.tinyurl.com/ContribHoliday

Step 3: Set up insurance – and a rainy day fund
Life insurance calculator: on www.consumer.org.nz
Savings account and bank deposit interest rates: www.interest.co.nz

Step 4: Join the best KiwiSaver fund for you

Which tax rate for your KiwiSaver account:
www.tinyurl.com/PIRratesNZ.

KiwiSaver first home help: www.tinyurl.com/
NZFirstHomeHelp

Online tools on KiwiSaver, retirement planning etc
www.sorted.org.nz

BBC podcast on index funds: www.tinyurl.com/BBCindex

Video on index funds: How to Win the Loser's Game on
www.youtube.com

KiwiSaver Tracker: www.tinyurl.com/KSTracker

Estimate of retirement spending: KiwiSaver Savings
Calculator on www.sorted.org.nz

Step 5: Boost your saving painlessly – how and where

Term deposit interest rates: Saving tab on www.interest.co.nz

What bonds are available: www.interest.co.nz

Credit ratings info: www.tinyurl.com/CreditNZ

Finding a financial service company's disputes resolution
scheme: www/tinyurl.com/NZRegister

Fake website set up by US government to warn scam victims:
www.howeycoins.com

Info on scams: www.consumeraffairs.govt.nz and click on
Scamwatch. Or www.fma.govt.nz and do a search for
'scams'

Step 7: Head confidently towards retirement – and through it

Lifespan calculator: www.tinyurl.com/ExpectLife

Info about rules of thumb on spending in retirement:
www.tinyurl.com/RulesOfThumbNZ

Tax if you have boarders or flatmates: www.tinyurl.com/
NZBoarderFlatmate

Rates postponement: www.tinyurl.com/NZPostponeRates.
    For Aucklanders: www.tinyurl.com/
    AuckRatesPostponement
Rates rebates: www.tinyurl.com/nzRatesRebate.
    For Aucklanders: www.tinyurl.com/AuckRatesRebate
Reverse mortgage calculator: www.seniorsfinance.co.nz

Step ?: (When it's the right time – if ever)
    Buy a home, or sell one
Info and to register an interest in KiwiBuild:
    www.kiwibuild.govt.nz
To get the rating valuation of a property: www.qv.co.nz
Info on properties: www.homes.co.nz
Mortgage break fee calculator: www.tinyurl.com/
    NZBreakFee
Mortgage calculator: www.sorted.org.nz
Mortgage rates: www.interest.co.nz
To compare long-term mortgage rates: www.tinyurl.com/
    NZMortgageRates
To check on a real estate agent's registration: www.rea.govt.nz

One more thing: Do you need personal financial advice?
Financial advisers who charge fees: Info on Advisers page on
    www.maryholm.com
John Oliver on Money: www.tinyurl.com/OliverMoney

On happiness
Compare NZ with other countries for wellbeing:
    www.oecdbetterlifeindex.org
Where you rank on world rich list: www.globalrichlist.com

Acknowledgments

The following people either read the book and gave me really helpful comments or told me True Tales: Craig Ansley, Tim Ansley, Diane Cheriton, Susan Cooper, Peter Daymond-King, Rennie Gould, Syd Holm, Pam Kershaw, Dominique Marriott, Chris Neilsen and Carol Painter.

Thanks, too, to Michael Chamberlain at MCA NZ for graphs and data for tables, and to the Reserve Bank of NZ and UMR research for permission to use their graphs.

At HarperCollins, thanks to publisher Alex Hedley for coming up with the idea for this book and for his guidance and encouragement.

Special thanks to Ian Tucker for his ongoing support and his frequent reminders that most things in life shouldn't be taken all that seriously.

Index